TAKEN FOR A RIDE

Taken for a Ride

The History of Cons and Con-men

Donald McCormick

HSP

HARWOOD-SMART PUBLISHING

First published in Great Britain 1976 by
Harwood-Smart Publishing Co. Ltd.
Wessex House, Blandford Heights, Blandford, Dorset
and
18 Coulson Street, Chelsea, London SW3 3NB

ISBN 0 904507 16 5

Printed in Great Britain by Chapel River Press, Andover, Hants.

Contents

1

PROPHETS, PRIESTS AND WOULD-BE KINGS

HOW TO define a con-man?

I would begin by saying that my use of the word is in no sense chauvinistic: there have been very many brilliant female confidence tricksters. If I must attempt a clear-cut definition of the con-man, I should like to make it within certain agreed limits. People will differ in their views of who is and who is not a con-man, probably depending on whether or not they have been the victim of one. This book is not an attempt to whitewash the con-man, but it is an effort to show that he or she is a person apart from the ordinary criminal practitioner of fraud.

While some con-men have been criminals, many have not. Quite a few have been brilliant practical jokers or fantasts. Among the very few have been visionaries and would-be prophets. Some of the lesser religions of the world have been the creations of con-tricksters.

So, to begin with, in this study of the con-man down the ages, I have tried to ensure that the selections made are of a certain standard and skill. It is not my purpose to sing a song in their praise, but I do aim to show that the true con-trickster has that "something extra" which in its way amounts to a spark of genius.

Of course, the border-line between the con-man and the mere criminal is a narrow one and in this area there is room for a great many differing opinions. But let us take an example from the Bible: one could say that Laban was a con-trickster when he substituted Leah for Rachel to consummate the marriage with Jacob under cover of darkness, but that Jacob's sons were merely crude criminals when they sold Joseph into slavery and then brought back his blood-stained clothes as "proof" that he had been killed by a wild beast.

The first con-tricksters of the ancient world were undoubtedly the oracles of ancient Egypt and Greece. Their particular speciality was a talent for making people believe that they could foretell the future and enable the world to be put in order. Not surprisingly, they came to be regarded as God's personal representatives on earth, though as a general rule they claimed to be the mouthpiece of some particular god. No wonder that Aristotle said that incredulity was the foundation of all wisdom, for its converse was certainly true. The oracles were quick to establish a kind of closed shop for prophecy-making and fortune-telling, setting up their own temples as consulting-rooms and taking care that they invested themselves with an air of mysticism.

Such was the reputation they enjoyed that every matter of importance was referred to them by heads of state, thus giving the oracles a powerful influence in the land and the opportunity to exploit their lucrative impostures far and wide. Nor was this entirely a one-way traffic by males. The master of a Phoenician vessel carried off a woman, an attendant of the temple of Jupiter, at Thebes, and sold her into slavery to barbarians in Thesprotia. But the woman was quick-witted enough to realise that her education gave her a distinct advantage over her captors and she decided to exploit this by playing on their ignorance. Telling them that she possessed the powers of prophecy known only to the Egyptian priests, she set herself up as an oracle under the branches of a spreading oak.

News of her supposed talents soon attracted many people to consult her. She claimed to be an oracle of Jupiter and established such a reputation for sagacity that legends sprung up about her. It was said that originally a black pigeon had flown from Thebes to Dodona and had proclaimed with a human voice that an oracle of Jupiter should be established there.

All manner of tricks were played by these priests and oracles in carrying out their "missions". There was, of course, a good deal of rivalry between the devotees of the different gods. The Chaldeans asserted that theirs was the strongest and most powerful of all gods. To demonstrate this they threw any symbols of rival deities into a fire which consumed them. A priest of Canopus, one of the Egyptian gods, decided to break this tradition of the power of the Chaldeans. He ordered an idol to be made of a very porous soil. Inside the belly of this idol he poured a vast quantity of water, having first made many little holes which, once the belly was filled, he sealed with wax. He then challenged the Chaldeans to put his idol to the test of fire. When they had prepared the fire he set his idol on top, bidding the Chaldeans to light it with their torches. As soon as the fire reached the wax, it dissolved, the holes were opened and the water poured out and extinguished the flames. This led to the belief that the god Canopus had destroyed the god of the Chaldeans. As a tribute to their victory the Egyptians forever after constructed their idols with large bellies.

That these early con-tricksters were ingenious and knowledgeable is certain. Rufinus tells us that when the Temple of Serapis at Alexandria was destroyed by order of Theodosius, it was found to be full of secret passages and many concealed gadgets and examples of primitive machinery intended to assist the impostures of the priests. On the eastern side of the temple, for example, there was a tiny window, through which, on a certain day of the year, the sunbeams shone on to the mouth of the statue of Memnon. On this day an iron image of the sun was brought into the temple. In the ceiling above was fixed a loadstone which caused the iron image of the sun to rise up to the statue of Memnon. The priests then claimed that the sun saluted their god. Many other similar tricks were practised on the credulous, one of them being to cause "sweet and melodious sounds" to issue from the statue's mouth. But no historian has explained how this was done, though Strabo claimed to have personally heard such sounds.

Astonishingly enough, the "priest" who practised the most ambitious and outrageous deception in early times was a woman. She has passed into legend as "Pope Joan" and posterity has commemorated her by a card game of that name, played with an ordinary pack of cards minus the eight of diamonds.

The origins of the mysterious Joan are somewhat vague. She lived in the ninth century and is said to have been born in England and educated at Cologne. As a young girl she lived in Mainz. There is no record of her until the first half of the thirteenth century when she was mentioned as Pope Joan by such chroniclers and preachers as the Dominican priests, Jean de Mailly and Stephen de Bourbon and the Polish Martin of Troppau. The last-named's account of Joan was the one which was most widely circulated and accepted. Martin declared that when Pope Leo IV died in 855, he was succeeded by a John Angelicus, who was really a woman, but who managed to stay in office for two and a half years as Pope John VIII.

The story about her, as told by these chroniclers, was that Joan fell in love with a young Benedictine monk and fled with him, disguised as a man, to Athens. It was then that she started calling herself John Angelicus. In Athens she studied ecclesiastical law and became quite an authority on the subject. She was returning to Mainz, still dressed as a man, when she stopped off at Rome, impressing everyone with her erudition. Given office as a Curial Notary, she achieved rapid promotion, eventually being made a Cardinal and, finally, elected Pope. Whether this was achieved through sexual influence as the mistress of the Emperor, one does not know, but it is significant that in this period the Emperors insisted on their right to confirm the election of the Pope.

Joan might have continued with her imposture for many more years, but for the fact that, while riding on horseback in a public procession, she was seized by labour pains. Some say she delivered the child in the road between the Colosseum and St. Clement's Church. Others say the child was born in the church. Her punishment and death are variously described, but the main impression is that she died in childbirth.

There is no documentation in the Vatican archives on Joan because its material only dates from the year 1000. While in modern times the Vatican and some ecclesiastical historians have done their utmost to discount the whole story of Pope Joan, inside the Vatican it was generally accepted as being true for some centuries. This is evident from the fact that Joan's statue was included among those of the Popes in the Cathedral of Siena (1400). During the reign of Pope Sixtus V a statuette of a mother and child was found in St. Clement's Church in Rome and this was believed to be of Pope Joan and her baby. The statuette is now in the Chiaromonti Museum.

The story of Pope Joan is a romance rich in possibilities and one would like to know what special qualities she brought to the Papacy, assuming that she existed and achieved temporary fame. It is not as improbable as modern historians suggest, for during the century following that of Joan there is considerable evidence of female influence around the Papacy and Benedetto of S. Andrea of Soratte wrote at that time that "the Church of Rome was in the hands of a woman". On the other hand, even if Joan did not become Pope, then someone in the thirteenth century pulled off a magnificent confidence trick which was accepted by the Vatican authorities.

The con-trickster is in his own sphere of action a craftsman, chiselling away at his imposture with all the skill and patience of a sculptor, introducing all the techniques of the actor. He is an artist to his finger-tips. Perhaps the female con-trickster is an even more consummate artist: certainly she often, as did Pope Joan and the temple attendant from Thebes, ventures into more audacious impersonations. The motivation for con-tricksters varies from vanity among the impostors to greed among the professional operators, while there have been con-men and women who have acted purely for patriotic reasons, or for some political cause. Others simply have a fondness for notoriety, or a desire to recreate a dream. Most of them have something of the Walter Mitty in their make-up. Thus it is that a study of credulity down the ages, and the way it has been exploited, shows that sometimes this has been so effective that the con-tricksters themselves have passed into folk-lore and so become heroes rather than villains.

Among the latter have been some of the royal impostors—the would-be kings. A throne seemed a much more seductive prospect centuries ago than it may appear today, and in various ages and countries people have impersonated the descendants of sovereigns and, in some instances, deceased sovereigns themselves. During the Wars of the Roses the clash between the rival families of the House of York and Lancaster gave rise to several remarkable impostures on the part of the Yorkists. The Duke of York in the reign of Henry VI of England persuaded an Irishman named Jack Cade to impersonate Mortimer, Earl of March, a name that was popular with the masses. In a matter of days, Jack Cade achieved such success in this role that he raised an impressive and efficient army of 20,000 in the county of Kent. At the head of this force he marched on London, defeated a detachment of the King's army sent to meet him, and took possession of the capital.

Cade himself had served as a soldier in the French wars and it was on the strength of this experience that he assumed the mantle of a general. But his troops were unruly and, having arrived in London to be greeted with a considerable degree of goodwill, they proceeded to dispel this by looting. Slowly, the opposing forces came to grips with the insurgents and cunningly offered the latter a pardon, if they would agree to retire from London. This the insurgents agreed to do and left their leader in the lurch. Jack Cade fled to Sussex where he was overtaken and killed.

But Jack Cade hardly came into the first class of con-tricksters. A much cleverer imposture was carried out during Henry VIII's reign when, about the year 1486, a fictitious prince was created by Richard Simon, a priest. Lambert Simnel was the son of a baker, but a youth of attractive appearance, with a striking personality and a high degree of intelligence. Simon decided that, given a certain amount of education and grooming, he could be passed off as a prince, especially as he bore a remarkable resemblance to the imprisoned Edward Plantagenet, Earl of Warwick.

Perhaps the rascally priest was inspired to attempt this impersonation when the rumour was spread that Richard, Duke of York, second son of Edward IV, had secretly escaped from imprisonment. But it seems likelier that partisans of the House of York used the priest as their instrument for perfecting a carefully worked out plot. For Lambert Simnel revealed an extraordinary amount of detailed knowledge of the life and habits of the Earl of Warwick and this could only have been provided by people close to the royal family.

Simnel was first sent over to Ireland where there were many supporters of the House of York. He presented himself to Thomas Fitzgerald, Earl of Kildare, claiming his protection as the unfortunate Earl of Warwick. Simnel's story was eagerly accepted as being authentic and he was not only lodged in Dublin Castle, but crowned with a diadem taken from the statue of the Virgin Mary and publicly proclaimed king as Edward VI.

The next move was made by Henry VII back in England. Having heard what had happened in Ireland and knowing that this was an imposture, he ordered that the real Earl of Warwick should be taken from the Tower of London and paraded through the streets of London. This piece of public relations convinced the English that Simnel was an impostor, but in Ireland the people—noblemen and commoners—stubbornly stood by their "King" and insisted that it was Henry VII who had imposed on the English by producing a bogus Earl of Warwick. Simnel should have known that, while he could have held out indefinitely in Ireland, he stood little chance of success if he went to England. But Simnel decided to chance his luck, crossed the Irish Sea and saw his small force defeated near Stoke-on-Trent. He himself was taken prisoner. For once Henry VII was magnanimous. He pardoned Simnel and made him a scullion in the royal kitchen. This was an equally brilliant stroke of public relations, for it not only kept Simnel in a menial position, but made him entirely dependent on the King's mercy. One false move and his head would have been on the block. It would seem that Simnel learned his lesson, for later he was raised to the rank of a falconer in the royal service.

Henry VII was plagued with bogus claimants to the throne throughout his reign. Doubtless there were more of them than history has actually recorded, for this kind of imposture always encourages imitators. The latter, not being skilled con-tricksters, would not have got very far with their impersonations. It was the Duchess of Burgundy, the sister of Edward IV of England, who had put out the report that her nephew, Richard Plantagenet, Duke of York, had escaped from the Tower of London. This was done to pave the way for an attempt to have the young Duke impersonated. The Duchess's agents discovered a youth named Perkin Warbeck, who was chosen to play the part. Warbeck was said to have been the son of a renegade Jew of Tournay, who had lived in London during the reign of Edward IV.

Both the two Princes imprisoned in the Tower of London had, of course, long since died, having been smothered by pillows while they slept and buried at night so that their cruel fate had been kept secret. Thus it was not too difficult to exploit the theory that they might still be alive. Young Warbeck's father was in favour at Court (possibly he had acted as a moneylender or broker) and on the strength of this he had persuaded the King to stand as godfather to his son. But gossip hinted at another explanation for this. Some people had noted that when Perkin was a boy he looked remarkably like his Sovereign, and the suggestion was that the King, who was a notorious womaniser, had had an affair with Warbeck's wife. No doubt this titbit of gossip had reached the ears of the Duchess of Burgundy, who felt it was a ready-made answer to her quest for someone to impersonate the young Prince.

She herself undertook the task of grooming Warbeck for his role, after which he went to Ireland, which country, as was the case with Lambert Simnel, was chosen as the appropriate place for his first appearance as Richard, Duke of York. When he landed at Cork and introduced himself as a Prince of the royal blood, he had no difficulty in rallying around him a number of supporters. News of his reception in Ireland reached Charles, King of France, then about to wage war against Henry VII. The French monarch promptly invited Perkin to visit him in Paris. Here the impostor was received with all the honours due to an heir to the English throne and it is said that his bearing and pleasing personality made a remarkably good impression at the French court.

Once an imposture really gets under way its success usually snowballs: everyone wants to join in the newcomer's triumphant progress. So it was with Perkin Warbeck. His success in Cork and Paris caused some in England to make common cause with him. Sir George Neville, Sir George Taylor and a hundred others went to Paris to offer their services to him. This exodus from England so alarmed Henry VII that he immediately signed a treaty of peace with Charles of France, who, as part of the bargain, ordered Warbeck to leave his territory. The Duchess of Burgundy then came to his rescue by giving him protection at her own court, bestowing upon him the honour of the White Rose of England. It was a shrewd move which, to many people, clinched the authenticity of Perkin's claim to the throne on the grounds that the aunt could hardly mistake the personal identity of her nephew.

Perhaps the greatest service which Perkin Warbeck did for England was to alarm Henry VII sufficiently so that for the first time in her history the nation acquired a Secret Service. The King seriously set about creating an Intelligence Service specifically to sniff out plots by impostors and to obtain evidence against them. He sent spies abroad to infiltrate themselves among the Warbeck circle, bribing the pretender's retainers and servants and even his personal chaplain to give information against

Perkin. As a result of this, many of the conspirators and followers of Warbeck were caught, condemned and executed.

Warbeck, however, held out for much longer. He launched a landing in Kent, but was repulsed. Returning to Flanders, he next sailed to Cork, but found that the Irish had lost their enthusiasm for his cause. Undeterred by these failures, he went to Scotland where King James not only recognised him as "the true Prince", but gave him in marriage a near relation, Lady Catherine Gordon. James also assisted Warbeck with two incursions into England, but both of these failed. Perkin, who seemed to be particularly quick to recognise when he needed to change tack, then again turned his attention to Ireland. He left Scotland with four ships and eighty followers and tried in vain to enlist the support of the Earl of Desmond in Cork. Finally he landed in Cornwall, having heard that the people of that county were hostile to King Henry VII. Six thousand Cornishmen joined him and he led them as far as Exeter where he was repulsed by the citizens. Hearing that Henry's forces were close at hand, he escaped and sought refuge in the sanctuary of Beaulieu in Hampshire. On being promised a pardon, he surrendered, but he was treacherously betrayed and committed to the Tower. It is possible that Henry might have been as magnanimous with him as he was with Lambert Simnel, but the discovery of a plot between Warbeck and the Earl of Warwick to escape and lead a revolt against the King sealed his fate. Warbeck was executed.

Another country where a spate of royal impostors occurred was Portugal, where doubts as to whether Sebastian had really been slain at the Battle of Alcazarquivir resulted in no fewer than six attempts to impersonate that gallant but feckless monarch. Sebastian had led a Portuguese invasion of Morocco in 1578, curiously enough aided by a Moorish Pretender to the throne of

Fez. In a fierce encounter Sebastian's forces were defeated and he was killed, but such was the confusion afterwards and the legend of Sebastian's omnipotence that many refused to believe in his passing.

The most remarkable of the six Pretenders to the Portuguese throne was Gabriel de Spinosa, a pastry-cook from Madrigal, who had been coached in his part by an Augustine friar, Father Michael de los Santos, who had been chaplain to Don Sebastian. One of the principal reasons for the impersonation of Sebastian was that Philip of Spain had usurped Portugal and resentment against the Spaniards ran high. The friar was father confessor to a convent of nuns at Madrigal in which Donna Anna of Austria, niece of Philip of Spain, was an inmate. He introduced the pretended Sebastian to her and she was so impressed that she gave him some jewels to raise money. It was while he was trying to sell these that Gabriel de Spinosa was arrested as a thief. He and the friar were executed and the Princess Donna Anna was removed to another convent and rigorously confined for the rest of her life.

Yet it has been in Russia that by far the most remarkable, and to some extent the most successful, con-tricks have been attempted in a bid to impersonate deceased princes. So frequent have such impostures been over the ages that they became almost a tradition of Russian life. It has occurred again in modern times and may well explain the Bolsheviks' real fear in the early days of the Revolution that someone would impersonate the last of the Czars, or his son.

The most successful of these Russian impersonators was a monk named Otrefief, who bore an astonishing likeness to Dmitri, younger son of the much-feared Czar, Ivan the Terrible. Ivan was succeeded as Czar by his elder son, Feodor. When Feodor, a particularly weak ruler, died, the throne was occupied by Boris Godunoff, who had been one of Ivan's closest associates and had married Ivan's sister. Boris had paved the way to his seizure of the throne by plotting the murder of the next in line, Dmitri. At first he was a highly successful monarch, winning over the boyars in 1597, completing the conquest and colonisation of Siberia and founding a university in Moscow. But towards the end of his reign, famine and plague created enormous suffering and hardship in Russia and Boris' popularity waned. It was then that Otrefief sought to exploit the situation by posing as the murdered Dmitri.

Because of the extraordinary likeness to the dead prince, Otrefief had little difficulty in persuading people, especially enemies of Boris, that he was the prince and had escaped from a murderous attack. A contemporary description of Otrefief said he was "possessed of qualities well calculated to win the suffrage of the crowd, for his figure was fine, his manners prepossessing and his eloquence forcible". The story he told was that he had been saved from Boris' assassins by the substitution of another youth in his place. He then went to Poland to seek allies. Promises of aid began to come to him from many parts. Sendomir, a wealthy noble, promised Otrefief his daughter in marriage whenever he became Czar; the Polish king supported him. In 1604, at the head of a small army of Cossacks and Poles, the impostor marched into Russia to meet the far larger force which Boris sent to meet him. The impersonating monk showed a surprising talent for generalship. He inspired his troops and revealed both great personal courage and a talent for tactics. Very soon Boris found that the fame of the imposter had caused many of his own troops to desert him. In despair he committed suicide by taking poison and Otrefief under the name of Prince Dmitri entered Moscow and was duly crowned Czar.

The imposter started well and gave every promise of being an able and popular Czar, making himself accessible to his lowliest subjects and listening to their tales of woe. This did not, however, endear him to the nobles, and Otrefief erred in allowing power to go to his head and lavishing honours on the Poles who had assisted his cause. The Russians detested Polish influence at the court. A counter-revolution was launched by Prince Schisky, the royal palace was stormed and the bogus Czar was killed.

2

WIFE-SWAPPING BY COMMAND OF THE ANGELS

MILITARY CONFIDENCE tricks and con-manship by generals have been practised from the Siege of Troy to the case of "The Man Who Never Was"—the extraordinary deception of the Germans in World War II by the planting of a dead body with bogus papers in his uniform on a Spanish beach.

In fact, con-manship is in many respects an essential military art, which all goes to show that what may be regarded as bizarre behaviour, downright roguery or even a criminal act in some circumstances can be respectable enough to earn an honour in a war situation. Without con-tricksters of both sexes armies, navies and air forces would be vulnerable and Secret Services rendered almost powerless. Thus, while the typical and natural con-trickster is essentially an individualist, the State will always try to recruit from his ranks and seek to channel his or her talents into its service.

One of the simplest, but most brilliant con-tricks in the military sphere was that perpetrated by Lord Norwich during the wars between Edward III of England and Philip of France. Angoulême was in English hands and had been bravely defended against tremendous odds by the Governor, Lord Norwich. But the Duke of Normandy had forced the English almost to the point of surrender. To avoid this, Norwich appeared on the garrison walls and requested an interview with the Duke of Normandy.

"I suppose you wish to surrender to me," said the Duke.

"No," replied Lord Norwich, "but as tomorrow is the feast of the Virgin, to whom I know that you, sir, as well as myself, bear a great devotion, I desire a cessation of arms for that day."

This proposal was agreed between the two men. Next day Lord Norwich ordered his men to pack their baggage and then marched them out of the garrison in the direction of the French camp.

The French forces, believing they had been betrayed and were about to be attacked, rushed to their arms, but Norwich sent a messenger ahead of his men, reminding the Duke of their agreement. Perhaps such a trick would not succeed today. The paradox is that, though this generation may superficially seem more compassionate and civilised, it lacks that quality of chivalry which distinguished the Middle Ages. The Duke of Normandy was piqued at having been tricked, but he kept his bargain not to molest the English forces. "I see the Governor has outwitted me," he commented, "but let us be content with gaining Angoulême."

The English troops were allowed to pass through the ranks of the French army without any hindrance.

In the fifteenth and sixteenth centuries, however, a new style of con-trickster evolved. This was the "spiritual" trickster who claimed to be able to communicate with the spirit world, to talk with angels and sometimes even with devils. In this age magic, as far as the general public was concerned, embraced both scientific experiment and superstitious pacts with the Devil. The man-in-the-street made little distinction between one and the other. On the continent of Europe there was an attempt to separate what the Renaissance occulists called white, or natural magic, from the black or diabolical kind.

John Dee was one of the very few English scientists who tried to copy the continental principle and made a quest for what he called "thaumaturge, or Divine Magic." This quest he defined as the search for the "communion with goode angels by purifyinge of the soul", but he warned that such a search could be foolish and dangerous if attempted by ignorant or unscrupulous people. He believed in astrology, which he found mathematically accurate and satisfying.

Yet despite these warnings to others, Dee himself was ruthlessly conned when he began seriously to take up crystal-gazing, or scrying as it was then known. He insisted that all he did was to practise crystalomancy as a means by which the spiritual part of him could be awakened and put into communication with the spiritual world. But he had no special talent for scrying himself and depended upon professional scryers.

In 1581 Dee found such a scryer in the person of one Barnabas Saul, a young lay-preacher who had become an occultist. In his diary of 9 October, 1581, Dee noted that "Barnabas Saul, lying in the . . . hall, was strangely trubled by a spirituall creature abowt midnight."

It was not long before Dee discovered that Barnabas Saul had a criminal record and, though he was prepared to overlook this on the grounds that Saul was too valuable a scryer to lose, it soon became apparent that the man was thoroughly unreliable. Soon afterwards Saul was charged with sorcery.

Dee, who among other things was astrologer to the Queen, a geographer and mathematician, next engaged the services of one Edward Talbott who had for some time been trying to supplant Saul as a scryer. He had told Dee that a spirit had informed him that Saul had been deceiving his master. These tactics proved successful, for within a few days of Saul's departure, Talbott had persuaded Dee to take him on a a scryer at a salary of £50 a year with free board and lodging, a comparatively well paid post by Elizabethan standards.

One cannot even be sure that Edward Talbott was this scryer's real name. When he entered Dee's service he adopted the name of Kelley and there is no record as to how or why he made this change. It was probably in an attempt to make a new career for himself and to cover up a criminal record. Little is known of Kelley's earlier life, but what records exist suggest that he had always been engaged in dubious activities. He was born at Worcester in 1555 and William Lilly, the seventeenth century astrologer, declared that one John Evans told him that "he was acquainted with Kelley's sister in Worcester, that she showed him some of the gold her brother had transmuted and that Kelley himself was an apothecary in Worcester".

Whether in his early days Kelley seriously believed he could find a formula for manufacturing gold, or if he was simply intent on convincing other people that he could transmute metals is a matter of conjecture. But his later career suggests that the transmutation of base metals into gold was a trick he constantly sought to play in order to gain power and influence. Before he met Dee he had travelled widely in England and Wales, leading a vagabond type of life during the course of which he had indulged in some sinister and necromantic practices. He had also been a forger and coiner and had had his ears cropped for this offence. The black skull cap he wore was intended to hide his shorn ears. An account of one of his adventures was given in a seventeenth century book, *Ancient Funerall Monuments*, by John Weever. This tells how Kelley put into practice "the diabolical questioning of the dead for the knowledge of future accidents."

This took place in the park of Walton-le-Dale in Lancashire and Weever wrote that when "the black ceremonies of the night ended, Kelley demanded of one of the gentleman's servants what corpse was the last buried in Law Church-yard, a church thereunto adjoining, who told him of a poor man who was buried there but the same day. He . . . entreated this foresaid servant to go with them to the grave of the man so recently interred, which he did; and withal did help them to dig up the carcase of the poor caitiff, whom by their incantations they made him (or rather some evil spirit through his organs) to speak, who delivered strange predictions concerning the same gentleman."

While working for Dee, Kelley had to take care that he did nothing which even hinted at black magic, as his master's approach to the occult was strictly on what he called "a spiritual basis." Nevertheless, it is clear from Dee's own diaries that Kelley very often played tricks on him and that the "visions" he saw in the crystal were often merely the information he wished to fob off on Dee. He was obsessed with the idea of manufacturing gold and making himself a rich man and he was constantly using Dee's time to carry out laboratory experiments to achieve this.

Kelley would gaze into the crystal and then tell Dee what he saw and what the "angels" told him: the assumption always was that it was only the angels who spoke to Kelley. From his copious diary notes, compiled daily with great regularity over the years, it is clear that Dee diligently cross-examined the angels through Kelley, sometimes correcting their facts, and even their grammar, and denouncing any he regarded as "doubtful agents", that is to say, bogus or evil spirits.

Whatever doubts Dee had about Kelley, he continued to employ him and regarded the man as the best scryer available. Kelley had nothing like the erudition of Dee, but he had taken the trouble to study Agrippa's occult philosophy and he carefully disguised his previous interest in black magic by pretending to have a deep revulsion for what he called "demonic magic". A man of some charm and a certain amount of personal magnetism as well as a quick mind, he may also have had a somewhat mesmeric influence on Dee. For not only did Dee himself have doubts about Kelley, which unfortunately he later refuted, but his wife, Jane, took a dislike to Kelley from the very first day that he entered their home. She had a premonition that Kelley would bring disaster on the family.

From Dee's diaries it is possible to build up a picture of how the "angelic conversations" were conducted. Kelley would kneel before Dee's crystal, praying that "sight might be given him therein", while Dee, a little apart from his colleague, invoked "the help of God and his good creatures for the furtherance of action." In one such instance Dee recorded with obvious excitement that after praying for sixteen minutes, Uriel the Spirit of Light appeared in the crystal.

There was one "angel" conjured up by Kelley to whom Dee took a special fancy. She appears again and again in his diary notes as a spirit-child, half-angel and half-elfin, "like a pretty girle of 7 or 9 yeares of age . . . with her hair rowled up . . . with a gown of Sey . . . she seemed to play up and down . . . and seemed to go in and out behind my bokes."

It was Kelley who introduced this "angel" to Dee. He said her name was Madimi, that she could speak several languages and had a remarkable memory. Dee wrote down in great detail all that Madimi was supposed to have told Kelley, and he noted that she appeared to them in visions for seven years and during this period grew in stature and maturity. There were other angels who provided a vast amount of information, including knowledge of a new language—Enochian. But Madimi remained the favourite of all the angels and the one to whom Dee was most prone to listen and with whom he had the greatest patience. The dictation of the Enochian language tried his temper sorely, for he spent a vast amount of time trying to decipher the symbols which eventually he brought into some kind of order so that an alphabet and grammar emerged. There is no reference to any such language or code prior to Dee's lifetime, though it was adopted by the Rosicrucian Order of the Golden Dawn in England about 1875. The mystery remains: did Kelley invent it? did he acquire it from some source before he met Dee? or was he possessed of some kind of telepathic gifts? Possibly the answer lies in an affirmative to each of these questions to some extent.

When Dee went to the continent at the invitation of Count Albertus Laski, a Polish nobleman, he was accompanied by his wife and family and Kelley and his wife. The Count had hoped that this pair of magicians would provide him with manufactured gold through their alchemical experiments, but Kelley quickly sensed that Laski was poor and that they ought to seek another patron. They travelled on to visit the Emperor Rudolph II of Bohemia in Prague, but fared no better financially, and before long returned to Poland to the court of King Stephen. Eventually they found a new patron in Count Wilhelm Rosenberg, Viceroy of Bohemia.

One day, when Dee and Kelley were scrying, Kelley suddenly seemed disturbed by what he saw in the crystal and declined to say what it was. Dee insisted that it was Kelley's duty to reveal all and hide nothing. Kelley replied that what he had seen and heard was "shocking and shameful" and he would prefer to remain silent. However, under constant pressure from Dee, he reluctantly agreed to tell all. According to Kelley, Madimi had appeared in the crystal and taken off her garments one by one until she was completely naked.

"Just as I have revealed all my innermost mysteries

to you," she said, "so all of you must reveal and share all with one another."

"What does she mean by that?" inquired Dee.

After some hesitation Kelley said he did not understand what Madimi meant.

"Then ask her," commanded Dee.

Kelley replied after further consultation with Madimi that she was urging them to "share all things in common and all things are to be in common between us, *including our wives*."

Dee ordered Kelley to give Madimi a stern rebuke and to ask her whether she was seriously suggesting God's commandments were to be broken. Or, as he hoped, did she simply mean that they should all share one another's tribulations?

"No," replied Kelley, "that was not the angel's intention. Madimi has made it quite clear that the sharing of the wives is to be on a physical as well as a spiritual basis. This is the will of God. I have tried to keep this from you and this is why in recent weeks I have tried to give up scrying, but you would not listen to me. Now we are both deeply involved."

From the record of Dee's diaries it is perfectly clear that ever since the pair had been on the continent Kelley had been reporting complaints from the angels that he had married the wrong woman against their commandments. Similarly, shortly before this revelation Kelley had shown increasing reluctance to undertake scrying. But all this may well have been a carefully planned build-up to the astonishing "command" of Madimi, for originally Kelley had claimed that the angels had urged him to marry when he himself was against the idea. Dee was, of course, horrified at the proposal and Kelley pretended to share this view.

It was at this stage that Madimi discarded that sweet innocence and playful manner she had formerly displayed and imperiously denounced Dee and Kelley as "fools of little understanding".

"Are you going to set yourselves up as Lord, Gods, Judges of the Heavens? Your own reason riseth up against my wisdom. Behold you are free. Do that which most pleaseth you."

The two men sat up until the early hours of the morning arguing about what they should do. Dee remained unconvinced for a long time, believing that his hitherto beloved Madimi must have become influenced by evil spirits. Kelley then sought to change Dee's mind by flattering him. "I find it harder than you to reconcile myself to the angelic commands," he said, "but that is because I lack your knowledge and wisdom in understanding the full meaning of these angelic messages. I am sure that you will be able to grasp this and explain to me what we ought to do."

By the time Dee went to bed his anger had given place to doubt and his resistance to the idea of what Madimi called "cross-matching" had begun to weaken. Describing in his diary how he informed his wife of the angelic command, he wrote: " 'Jane,' I said, 'I can see that there is no other remedy, but as hath been said, of our cross-matching, so it must need be,' "

Jane Dee was outraged by what she heard. She "fell aweeping and trembling for full a quarter of an hour, then burst forth into a fury of anger." Begging Dee never to leave her, she commented: "I trust that though I finde myself thus to be used that God will turn me into a stone before he would suffer me in my obedience to receive any shame or inconvenience . . . I shall eat neither fish, nor flesh until this action, so contrarie to the wholesome law of God . . . is confirmed."

She herself believed that an evil spirit must have been masquerading as a good angel, and insisted that Madimi or some other angel should make a sign if any mistake had been made.

But the angels gave no such sign and so a document

was drawn up and ratified and signed by Dee, Kelley and their respective wives on 3 May, 1587. This testified that they would each faithfully observe and carry out the angelic commands, with secrecy upon pain of death to any of the four:

"I, John Dee, Edward Kelley, and our two wives, covenanted with God and subscribed the same, for indissoluble and inviolable unities, charity and friendship keeping between us four, and all things between us to be common as God by sundry means willed us to do."

There would seem to be little doubt that these "angelic commands" were entirely the invention of Kelley and that he had plotted the whole affair of wife-swapping for his own ends. For some time he had expressed an admiration for Jane Dee and sometimes compared his own wife with her in unfavourable terms. But there may have been another reason for the proposal. Though Dee himself had never mixed up scrying with sex rites, there had since the earliest times been a tradition that a sex rite or sacrifice in some way brought the crystal-gazer in closer touch with the spirit world. While lusting after Jane Dee, is it possible that Kelley subscribed to this theory?

From the wording of the document that they all signed it is clear that both men had a hand in the phrasing of the petition, but the handwriting is that of Dee, so one must assume that he accepted full responsibility for it. Yet when it came to the moment for partners to be exchanged, it was Kelley who feigned to draw back from the arrangement. This may have been a wily move by him to persuade Jane Dee that he was even more reluctant than her husband to follow the angels' bidding. He told her: "My heart pales at the arrangement, but your husband is made of sterner stuff. He is persuaded it is right."

From this one may surmise that Jane Dee still persisted in expressing vehemently her horror at the idea of having to share her bed with Edward Kelley. Nor was she taken in by Kelley's protestations that it was with a sad heart he undertook this angelic command. On 6 May, 1587, Dee laid the document of their covenant on the south table of the chapel in Rosenberg's palace and then offered up many prayers for divine guidance as to what they should do next.

But what *did* happen next? There are no records to show how the experiment in wife-sharing was conducted. It seems probable that the exchange of partners was a dismal failure. The only shred of evidence we have is that of Kelley himself, notoriously an unreliable witness. He declared that on 7 May he took the document of their petition, tore it into small pieces, destroyed it and then went off with one of the crystals used for scrying. This was eventually found under Jane Dee's pillow, but whether she or Kelley put it there is not known. Could it have been that she wanted to stop Kelley from further scrying and so from obtaining more instructions from the angels? Or had she wished to experiment in scrying herself?

What is certain is that as from this date the scrying ceased. Madimi made her last appearance to Dee and Kelley in May, 1587. After that the "angelic conversations" ended and there is no further account of them in Dee's book on the subject, his *Liber Mysteriorum*.

The whole mysterious affair of wife-swapping came to an end apparently on 19 July, 1587, when Dee noted in his diary: "A certayn kinde of recommendation between our wives. Next day saw relenting of E.K., also by my Lord's entreaty."

From then on Kelley became very much independent of Dee. He employed a man named John Carprio to build furnaces for his alchemical experiments and he was joined by his brother, Thomas. Sometime after this, Kelley set himself up in apartments of his own in the Rosenberg palace, at the same time undermining Dee's influence with Rosenberg by hinting that his master wasted his time in unprofitable ventures and researches. Kelley also sent messages to London, stressing that he was on the verge of manufacturing gold. At this time there was an almost hysterical demand for gold at the English Court, as, short of funds, preparations were made for the Home Fleet to face the Spanish Armada. The news that the Spanish Plate Fleet had returned from the West Indies with a cargo of sixteen million ducats in gold had made men greedy at the English Court. Kelley sought to fan these dreams of gold by manufacturing it in sufficient quantities to satisfy their needs.

With this idea in mind, and in the hope that he could persuade Elizabethan statesmen to accept his alchemical experiments as *bona fide*, Kelley sent his brother Thomas to London to plead his cause. He had won over the favours of the gullible Rosenberg and was now addressed by Englishmen as "Sir Edward Kelley", though his title was really that of a barony of the Kingdom of Bohemia, conferred on him through the influence of Rosenberg. His brother told Lord Burghley that Kelley had been able to manufacture an ounce of gold from an ounce and a quarter of mercury. Burghley thereupon sent a message to the Queen's agent in Prague, telling him to ask "Sir Edward Kelley to come over to his native countrie and honour Her Majestie with the fruites of such knowledge as God has given him."

Meanwhile, Kelley's feverish experiments were not producing gold in the quantities he had promised and both Rosenberg and the Emperor Rudolph became impatient. The English Lord Treasurer, Burghley, bluntly put Kelley to the test, suggesting that he should "send Her Majestie as a token a good round sum of money, say enough to defray the expenses of the Navy for the summer."

"Many say that if you come not, it is because you cannot perform what has been reported of you," wrote

Burghley. "I am expressly commanded by Her Majestie to require you to have regard to her honour . . . be assured of worldly reward, you can make your Queen so happie . . . surely as no subject she hath can do the like. Good Knight, let me end my letter, conjuring you in God's holy name not to keep God's gift from your natural countrie, but rather helpe make Her Majestie a glorious and victorious power againste the mallyce of hers and God's enemies."

But Kelley's only real achievement seems to have been the creation of some bogus gold out of part of a warming-pan! The truth is that he knew perfectly well that he could not possibly produce gold in the quantities demanded of him and he was afraid to return home and admit failure. From this date his luck left him. The Emperor Rudolph had him flung in prison on a charge of sorcery. When he was released he lived on his wits, wandering across the continent from one country to another, sometimes casting horoscopes and still pretending to manufacture gold to anyone who would listen to him. On the continent he was almost totally discredited, however, though he wrote letters to England still boasting of the gold he could create. One Philip Gawdy, writing to his brother in 1593, states that "Kelley is delivered out of prison and restored to his former estate and maketh gold as fast as a hen will cracke nuttes."

A few years later he was back in prison. His end remains a mystery, but it is said that he lost his life when trying to escape by making his bedclothes into a rope. Other reports say he was killed in prison. Part knave, part-self-deluder, Kelley was nevertheless a man of some ability and scholarship. He undoubtedly had some mystical talents in the field of what today we should call telepathy or extra-sensory-perception. Possibly, too, he indulged in the taking of primitive drugs, perhaps of aconite and deadly nightshade, the Elizabethan equivalent of LSD.

3

THE GIRL WHO GAVE BIRTH TO RABBITS

CON-MANSHIP IN the seventeenth and eighteenth centuries changed in style considerably. It became both more original and more outrageous.

In the seventeenth century various astrologers emulated the feats of Edward Kelley, though they drew the line at trying to manufacture gold, a ploy which had swiftly lost all credence. They found a lucrative source of income in being consulted by persons in quest of lost property and, especially during the Civil War in England, in forecasting the results of battles. William Lilly was consulted during this period both by the Royalists and the Parliamentary Rebels as a caster of horoscopes for political purposes. He was one of the first astrologers to be called in by the military not only to forecast the likely trends of campaigns, but also to help in psychological warfare. General Fairfax called upon him to address his troops in prophetic terms intended to encourage their belief in his astrological talents.

Gradually astrology came to be regarded in a number of countries as something respectable, honest and even scientific and so its practitioners ceased to be contricksters. As soon as the astrological text-book appeared on the scene, the scope for the trickster was drastically reduced.

Towards the end of the year 1726 one of the most extraordinary impostures ever attempted was carried out by a woman named Mary Toft, the wife of a journeyman cloth-worker at Godalming in Surrey. It was Mary Toft's stupidity and her inability to read or write which caused so many people to believe in her. They could not imagine how anyone as dull-witted as she was could possibly deceive them.

For Mary Toft claimed that she had given birth to rabbits. She explained this away by saying that as she was weeding in a field, a rabbit sprang up near her and after that she had a longing for rabbits. She was vague as to whether the rabbit actually had physical contact with her, but a contemporary account states that soon afterwards another rabbit sprang up near her in the same place, "which she endeavoured to catch. The same night she dreamed that she was in a field with two rabbits in her lap, and awaked with a sick fit, which lasted till morning; from that time for above three months she had a constant and strong desire to eat rabbits, but being very poor and indigent, could not procure any."

It may seem even more extraordinary that in the eighteenth century (the age of reason) anyone should believe the story of a woman giving birth to rabbits, yet Mary Toft actually deluded her own doctor, a Mr. Howard, a man of sound reputation who had practised medicine for more than thirty years. He believed that within a month he had personally helped her to produce nearly twenty rabbits from her womb. Once the local doctor supported such a story, of course, the news of this sensation travelled far and wide. It even reached the Court where King George I was so fascinated that he ordered his house surgeon, Mr. Ahlers, to go down to Godalming to investigate. Ahlers duly returned to London and expressed himself as being satisfied that this was indeed the truth and that Mary ought to be awarded a royal pension.

Mr. St. André, surgeon and anatomist to the King, was

then sent to make a further examination, as George I was not only keenly interested in the case, but anxious to consider granting a pension to Mary. St. André also went back to the Court fully convinced he had every proof that the story was true. He brought back one of the rabbits alleged to have been born to Mary and actually dissected it in front of the King. From that moment, what had hitherto been only gossip confined to relatively few people suddenly appeared in the press. A fierce controversy raged between those who believed the story and those who refused to accept the evidence. The King was strongly inclined to support the believers, while the Queen was foremost among the doubters and it was largely through her intervention that the affair was finally unmasked and Mary Toft lost the chance of a pension.

Some insisted it was a miracle. One man wrote a pamphlet claiming that what had happened to Mary Toft was simply the confirmation of a prophecy in the books of Esdras. But Hogarth, the painter and cynic, satirised the whole affair in cartoons and in an engraving called *Cunicularii*, or "The Wise Men of Godalming".

It was the Queen who sought the services of Sir Richard Manningham, a Fellow of the Royal Society and of the College of Physicians in London. Manningham then set out to examine the woman and afterwards made his detailed report on her which was printed afterwards under the title of *An Exact Diary of what was observ'd during a Close Attendance upon Mary Toft, the pretended Rabbit-Breeder of Godalming*.

Telling how he found Mary Toft sitting in a great chair by the fireside, Manningham said : "I asked her if she was then in pain, she answered no, but that she had some sharp pains just before I came in. I then touch'd her and in the vagina perceiv'd with my forefinger and thumb somewhat like a piece of skin . . . I presently took took out what lay in the vagina, and upon examining it, confess I was much surpris'd, it appearing to me so like a piece of hog's bladder that I was not able to form any other judgment of it."

His suspicions aroused, Manningham then decided to bring Mary Toft to London, lodging her at "Mr. Lacy's bagnio in Leicester Fields." For a few days she still professed to have labour pains, Then one Thomas Howard, porter at the bagnio, made a statement on oath before a magistrate concerning a rabbit which Mary Toft had obtained with his assistance. On the strength of this the woman was taken into custody and cross-examined further. Finally, she broke down and confessed that the whole affair had been a fraud. But Manningham was more concerned with the need to effectively kill the story and the gossip than to punish Mary Toft. He wrote: "I think Mary Toft should by no means be sent to prison, till the truth comes out, but that she should rather be kept and most strictly watched in some private house, where all persons, those of the Faculty especially, may have free and convenient access to her, which a prison will not so well afford, till the matter be as plainly and fully detected as possible."

In short, Manningham was most concerned that the medical profession themselves should be convinced of the fraud, which is not in the circumstances surprising. When the woman eventually made her confession she admitted that in conspiracy with another woman she had perpetrated this fraud as a "way of getting a very good livelihood." There is no doubt that she expected to gain many gifts and possibly a pension, if she could only keep up the legend of producing rabbits long enough.

Sir Richard Manningham wrote that her accomplice told her that "she must put up her body so many pieces of rabbits as would make up the number of rabbits which a doe rabbit usually kindles at one time, otherwise she would be suspected. Mary Toft asked how many that was; the woman told her sometimes thirteen. From that time Mary Toft did often, by the assistance of that woman, convey parts of rabbits into her body till at last she could do it by herself, as she had an opportunity, and that she did continue so to do.

"Now, by the constant irritation of those extraneous bodies, thus artfully convey'd into her vagina, the whole uterus suffer'd much and became larger in bulk than it ought to be in its natural state; and the bones, and other parts of those rabbits, so convey'd into the vagina, did often offend the neck of the uterus, which together with artful management of herself did occasion those violent bearing-down pains, which came on by intervals, and very exactly counterfited the true labour pains. The motions of her belly were partly artifice and partly real convulsions."

The "miracle" which had ended in farce saw Mary Toft being commited to Tothill Fields, Bridewell, and the reputation of the two Court doctors was seriously impaired. Indeed, Dr. St. André himself was accused by some of being an impostor. His enemies referred to another peculiar incident in which he had been involved two years earlier. He had then been called to visit a patient he had never seen before and was led by a messenger one dark night through winding alleys to a house in a court. There, while he attended a woman, he was given some strong liquor which he swore had poisoned him. The Government, after prompting from the Court, offered a reward of £200 for the detection of the offender, but the culprit was never found. St. André's enemies now said he was a compulsive liar and that the incident was a figment of his imagination.

It is an interesting conjecture as to which came first—the saying "to produce the rabbit out of the hat", or Mary Toft's charade. But it could well be that the saying often heard in parts of rural England, "she couldn't even produce a rabbit" in relation to a childless woman, has its origin in the strange events at Godalming.

In 1757 a certain Mr. Kent became enamoured of his late wife's sister, Fanny. She came to look after him and two years later they took lodgings together in the house of one Parsons, the clerk of St. Sepulchre's Church in Cock Lane, Smithfield.

One day, Kent made a long journey into the country to attend a wedding to which he had been invited. Fanny, not wishing to be left entirely alone in the house, asked the twelve-year-old daughter of the landlord, Elizabeth Parsons, to share her bed. In the early hours of the morning they were awakened by the sound of strange rappings and scratchings. They thought the cause of these noises must be a neighbouring cobbler.

Perhaps at that time the cobbler was the culprit, but later, when Fanny again heard the noises, she noticed they occurred on Sundays as well, days on which the cobbler never worked. Fanny then began to form the notion that the noises were a supernatural warning of her impending death. Kent himself could not dispel this idea from her mind, so the couple moved to Bartlett Court, Clerkenwell, where on 2 February, 1760, Fanny died of smallpox, according to the certificate of her physician.

Eighteen months later the mysterious noises in the house in Cock Lane started up again. They seemed to come from the bed of Elizabeth Parsons, who also claimed that she had been confronted in the middle of the night by the apparition of a woman surrounded by a blazing light. When questioned, she thought the apparition resembled Fanny, and that the ghost of the dead woman was trying to tell her she had been murdered.

Mary Fraser, a nurse who had been called in to attend to Elizabeth Parsons, suggested they should question the apparition the next time it appeared. The knockings and rappings had now become louder and more persistent and the news that the Cock Lane house was haunted had begun to spread in the vicinity. It was agreed that a number of men, including a clergyman, should sit by the bedside of Elizabeth Parsons with a view to questioning the ghost when it appeared. One man pointed out that ghosts do not usually talk and that the probable means of communication would be by rappings, so it was suggested that when the ghost appeared, or if the rappings were heard, they should convey to the ghost that a code should be established for answers to their questions—one knock for "yes" and two for "no".

This procedure was carried out when the rappings began and the answers the watch party obtained were that the ghost was that of Fanny and that she had been poisoned with red arsenic in a glass of purl. It is difficult to see how they could have obtained such details as these solely through rappings and this may have been an embellishment of their story, but clearly they were satisfied that this was Fanny Kent's ghost, or someone who was impersonating her. As some of the watchers suspected an imposture, Elizabeth Parsons was taken away from her home and put to bed in several houses during the next week or two. The number of watchers was increased to twenty, this time including ladies and another clergyman. Yet still the rappings and scratchings continued at the house in Cock Lane and the same answers were given to the questions—that this was the ghost of Fanny and that she had been murdered.

During one of these sessions one of the watchers put this question to the ghost: "We want some positive proof that you really are the spirit of Fanny. Will you attend upon one of us in the vault in St. John's Church, where she is buried, tomorrow night?"

A single rap affirmed that it would.

"Will you then manifest your presence to us by giving a knock upon the coffin?"

Again the answer was "yes".

By this time the story of the Cock Lane ghost had reached even the fashionable houses of London. Horace Walpole, always a lover of scandal, wrote to Sir Horace Mann: "I am ashamed to tell you that we are again dipped into an egregious scene of folly. The reigning fashion is a ghost—a ghost that would not pass muster in the paltriest convent in the Appenines. It only knocks and scratches: does not pretend to appear or to speak. The clergy give it their benediction: and all the world, whether believers or infidels, go to hear it. I, in which number you may guess, go tomorrow."

It is recorded that Walpole went to the house in Cock Lane with the Duke of York, Lady Northumberland, Lady Mary Coke and Lord Hertford. He noted that "the house is wretchedly small and miserable. When we opened the chamber, in which were fifty people with no light but one tallow candle at the end, we tumbled over the bed of the child to whom the ghost comes, and whom they are murdering by inches in such insufferable heat and stench . . . they told us (as they would at a puppet-show) that it would not come that night until seven in the morning . . . we stayed, however, until half an hour after one."

Among the small party that went to the vaults of St. John's Church was the great Dr. Samuel Johnson himself. "The spirit was then very seriously advertised that the person to whom the promise was made of striking the coffin was then about to visit the vault, and that the performance of the promise was then claimed. The company at one o'clock went into the church and the gentleman to whom the promise was made went with another into the vault. The spirit was solemnly required to perform its promise, but nothing more than silence ensued."

During this period, the wretched man Kent had been subjected to all kinds of villification and he had been openly accused of murdering Fanny. Fortunately, he was able quite easily to prove his innocence by obtaining certificates of the cause of Fanny's death from both his physician and apothecary.

Once this was done, suspicion began to fall increasingly on Elizabeth Parsons. Her bed was slung like a hammock in the middle of her room and she was closely watched during the night. Rappings and scratches were still heard, but when she was bound hand and foot in the hammock, all was silence. By then the watchers were convinced that Elizabeth Parsons was the cause of all the rappings and scratchings. They then sought to trap her by asking her to summon the ghost at six o'clock in the morning. Perhaps she thought that by that hour they would be too sleepy to appreciate that they were being tricked. But in the morning, when the sounds were heard again, they asked her if she had concealed in the bed any piece of wood. This she denied, but when they stripped her bed the watchers found a small wooden board hidden under Elizabeth Parsons' stays.

The child was not the real culprit, but only the instrument of her father, mother and the nurse Fraser, all of whom were indicted at the Guildhall. Apparently Kent had lent Parsons some money some years previously and, after patiently waiting for repayment for a long time, had been forced to go to law to recover it. Ever afterwards Parsons had nurtured a hatred for Kent and had been determined to blacken his character. It was his plan to get his daughter to go along with the story of the Cock Lane ghost. Possibly, once the charade had got under way, Parsons realised that his family could derive some benefit by maintaining it permanently, for Horace Walpole wrote that the Methodists had promised the Parsons family contributions. "Provisions are sent in like forage, and all the taverns and alehouses in the neighbourhood make fortunes."

Parsons was sentenced to be placed three times in the pillory at the end of Cock Lane and to be confined for two years in the King's Bench Prison. His wife was given a year's imprisonment and the nurse, Mary Fraser, six months. Yet, curiously, this family's dastardly plot to smear Kent's reputation never seems to have aroused any hostility. When Parsons was in the pillory nobody threw things at him or in any way insulted him and afterwards a public subscription was raised for his benefit. As for Elizabeth Parsons, she married twice and lived until she was sixty-two.

Perhaps the hoax aroused a certain amount of sneaking admiration among those who did not know that the original purpose of the imposture was to ruin Kent. But it also seems possible that many believed that there really was a ghost in the house in Cock Lane, despite the trial of the Parsons. Nor was this merely the view of the ignorant and superstitious. Andrew Lang, the historian and literary critic, who made a study of the supernatural, wrote a book entitled *Cock Lane and Common Sense* in which he suggested that the story of the rappings and scratchings was not entirely an imposture.

4

SOUTH SEA BUBBLE

COLONIAL EXPANSION among the great powers of Europe in the eighteenth century led to the creation of a large number of joint stock companies concerned with overseas development. They provided a new medium for the con-trickster and those who sought to raise false hopes about speedy means of making fortunes.

"Bubble" was the name given to all these extravagant projects for which subscriptions were raised and negotiated at vast premiums in Change Alley. Indeed bulls and bears, those terms now so common on the Stock Exchange, are a legacy of these days. He who sold that of which he was not yet possessed was proverbially said to have sold the skin before he had caught the bear.

The most notorious of all these extravagant enterprises was, of course, the South Sea Bubble. Such was the belief in this scheme that hundreds of people from the highest to the lowest firmly believed that this project put El Dorado within every man's grasp.

The South Sea Company originated in the reign of Queen Anne in the year 1711, a fund being raised on the supposition that the English would be allowed to trade along the coast of Peru. In the beginning, the main object of this operation was that Harley, the Lord

Treasurer, wished to have taken up the large floating debt which the War of the Spanish Succession (1710-13) had created. The Company of Merchants of Great Britain was then granted exclusive rights of trading on the east and west coasts of South America and all lands which it might discover within 300 leagues from the shore were to be held by the company under the Crown.

In 1714, by the further transformation of government debts, the capital stock was increased to £10,000,000, while in 1719 the directors of the company proposed to absorb the whole national debt and pay five per cent interest for seven years and four per cent thereafter. For this privilege they offered £7,567,000. Any close examination of the project and the realisation that the company had done very little trading should have deterred enthusiasts for the stock, but the public were misled partly by the support which the Government gave to the company and partly by the manipulations of a few financial con-tricksters. So they rallied in their hundreds to support the scheme in the belief that the boom would extend to the South Seas and speculation carried the stock to £1,000 for every £100 subscribed.

The man who originally put the scheme on the map was Sir John Blunt, who set the idea before the Chancellor of the Exchequer. But he had really copied the Mississippi Plan which had been launched in 1719 by John Law, of Lauriston, an adventurous and imaginative financier from Edinburgh. Law had great talents and flair as an entrepreneur, but in his own way was a mesmeric con-man. Early in life he had fought a duel in which he killed his opponent and because of this was forced to flee to the continent. He settled in Paris, and in 1718 induced the Regent of Orleans to adopt his suggestion for a national bank. Law's proposal, which ultimately ruined thousands of families in France, was the creation of a royal bank through subscriptions. Out of this project developed the Mississippi Scheme by which Law's Louisiana Company absorbed the Canada Company and acquired rights over the whole territory drained by the Mississippi, Missouri and Ohio Rivers. Law's plan envisaged a vast colonisation of these territories, the purchase of the tobacco monopoly and the absorption of the East India, China and Senegal Companies. To be fair, the project was not only ambitious, but had something substantial to offer, but Law soon found himself to be the dupe of the Regent, who transferred the burden of 1,500 million francs of the King's debt on to the shoulders of the people.

It is perhaps a moot point as to who was the biggest con-trickster—Law or the Regent. The Louisiana Company in effect had under its control the management of the Mint, all colonial trade, and the finance and currency of France. Shares in the company rose higher even than England's South Sea Bubble and in 1720 Law became Controller-General of the national finances and attempted to amalgamate the company with the *Banque Royale*. He was about to become the most powerful man in France, but by one of those quirks which can affect even the soundest schemes, public confidence suddenly wilted when the amalgamation scheme was known. There was a run on the bank and panic ensued. Finally the bank stopped payment. The Regent, who in many respects was primarily to blame, allowed Law to become the political scapegoat for the failure of the Mississippi Scheme. He was forced to flee from France and he died in poverty in Venice.

Sir John Blunt intended to emulate the Mississippi Scheme, but he had nothing like the same prospects of material wealth which Law could offer. However, he thought that he could profit from the errors of the French project and, by skilful manoeuvring, lure a gullible public into believing that they could make a fortune out of the South Sea Company. But the South Sea Scheme promised no commercial advantage of any consequence: even the title "South Sea Company" was misleading for an organisation which had little to do with the "South Seas". It is true that in 1720 the company's monopoly was extended to what were known as the South Seas, but this in no way represented the truth.

Blunt was the father of all British con-tricksters. From the beginning he set out to deceive, to curry favour with the Government, to play on the rapacity and stupidity of individuals and to make mere tools of the other directors so that they served his own purposes. His ingenuity as a manipulator would have surprised even the most sophisticated gambler on the modern Stock Exchange. When he found the South Sea stock did not rise as far as his hopes, he invented reports that Gibraltar and Port Mahon would be exchanged for some places in Peru, by which means the company's trade would be increased. This story did the trick; speculators rushed in to buy stock and the directors opened their books for a subscription of one million pounds, at the rate of £300 for every hundered pounds of capital. The Stock Exchange was stampeded. Statesmen, clergymen, lawyers, physicians and all manner of professional people rushed in to subscribe to what had already become known as the "South Sea Bubble". The poet Gay had a present of some South Sea stock given to him and believed himself to be worth £20,000. His friends advised him to dispose of at least a part of the stock, but, certain that his £20,000 would grow until it was more than £100,000, he declined all such suggestions. Fenton, a close friend, told him: "Purchase an annuity of £100. That will make you sure of a clean shirt and a shoulder of mutton every day." In the end, Gay not only lost all the stock, but was almost totally ruined.

New companies were started every day, all linked to the South Sea Bubble. There were proposals to import asses from Spain (a delightful piece of imaginative cynicism!) and to extract silver from sea-water. One obscure projector put forward what he called "A Most Exceedingly Advantageous Scheme", which, however, he did not define or explain, but merely published proposals for a subscription, in which he promised that in one month the particulars would be disclosed. Meanwhile, explained the outrageous projector, "each person paying two guineas will be entitled to a subscription of one hundred pounds, which will produce that sum annually." In one afternoon the advertiser received a thousand subscriptions and that same night he shut up his doors and left the country.

One totally fictitious company which sprang up was called Globe, selling as "permits" square pieces of cardboard on which was a sealing-wax impression of the Globe Tavern. They were absolutely worthless, yet they changed hands at £60 a card.

Such madness in speculation could not possibly last. By September 8th, 1720 the stock began to falter. From then on there was a rush to get rid of it until by the end of the month the stock had sunk to £150. Some bankers and goldsmiths who had lent money were obliged to stop payment and absconded. Everywhere there were financial tragedies. Matthew Prior wrote in one of his letters a year before his death: "I am tired of politics and lost in the South Sea: the roaring of its waves and the madness of the people are justly put together."

The King, George I, was out of the country at the time of the crash and had to be brought back from Hanover. Parliament met and bills intended to cope with the financial crisis were passed, but the whole nation was engulfed by the repercussions of the South Sea Bubble. Knight, the treasurer of the South Sea Company, fled from the country and, though he was followed to the continent by agents of the Government, escaped arrest. He had been one of the subsidiary con-tricksters who implemented Blunt's plan. So vast were the ramifications of the South Sea Bubble, and so many were the tricksters who joined in the mad scramble for riches, that the complete story of this financial madness can never be told. But secret committees of investigation formed by Members of the House of Commons gradually unfolded a tale of villainy and imposture. A number of Ministers were involved and the Chancellor of the Exchequer was not only expelled from the House, but committed to the Tower. A resolution stated that he had "promoted the destructive execution of the South Sea scheme, with a view to his own exorbitant profit, and had combined with the directors in their pernicious practices, to the ruin of public credit".

From then on the word "Bubble" was applied to any and all extravagant projects for which subscriptions were raised. One contemporary commentator wrote that "the mania was so great at that time, that no fewer than 240 bubbles, of different descriptions, were blown by needy and knavish projectors, which shortly burst and left but a wreck behind".

Of all the con-tricks pulled during the era of "Bubble" speculation the most impudent was that cited by Maitland in his *History of London*. He referred to the establishment of a company "to make deal boards out of sawdust." But, on investigation, it would appear that Maitland himself was conned in this instance. There was no such company, but a burlesque or hoax appeared in the form of an advertisement in the press, stating that "on Tuesday next following . . . books will be opened for a subscription of two millions of pounds . . . for the invention of melting down sawdust and chips and casting them into clean, deal boards without knots".

While there is no evidence that any trickster made any money out of this, the advertisement still attracted a few gullible would-be subscribers.

In the eighteenth century there were more rascally clergymen of the Church of England than in any other age, many of them being hard-drinking, red-faced fox-hunting, gambling country vicars whose interests outside their churches were dubious to say the least. A number of these fox-hunting vicars, desperately anxious to get in on the "Bubble" band-wagon, set up a company for "encouraging the breeding of horses in England, and improving of glebe and church lands, and repairing and rebuilding parsonages and vicarage houses". The shares were speedily snapped up and probably many of their parishioners lost money.

Just how uninhibited were the gambling instincts of the British people in this period is illustrated by this advertisement, which was no joke at all, but a serious attempt to raise funds: "A company for carrying on an undertaking of great advantage, but nobody to know what it is." The sales talk of this plausible adventurer was that the details of the scheme required absolute secrecy for the time being and that such secrecy was imperative for the success of the venture. Half a million was the capital he required to raise and he asked for deposits of two guineas a share.

An office was duly opened in Cornhill and within a few hours a queue had formed. By the end of the afternoon the con-man of the century had netted more than £2,000. This was well short of his target of half a million, but enough to enable him to set off by coach for Dover and the continent, never to be seen in England again.

5

THE LADY-IN-WAITING WAS A MALE SPY

THE TALK and the toast of the young "gallants" at the Court of the Czarina Elizabeth in the mid-eighteenth century was a shy, but attractive lady-in-waiting generally known as Mam'selle Lia. In that roisterous and sometimes unruly Court the virginity of the ladies-in-waiting was not always easily preserved and any girl who held out against the advances of the bold young officers stood out not only as an exception, but as someone infinitely desirable.

Mademoiselle Lia de Beaumont had only been in St. Petersburg on a visit from Paris for a short while before she attracted the Czarina's attention. She was said to be a member of a very well connected French family, but few knew much about her except that her chaperon, most unusually, was not a Frenchwoman, but a Scots*man*—a Mr. Mackenzie Douglas, who claimed to be her uncle.

Painters begged for permission to execute portraits of Lia, often prefixing their requests to the Czarina in the most flattering terms: they wished to "capture her pink and white complexion", or to "save for eternity that sweet and gentle expression." One painter wanted to portray her as Aphrodite.

To understand how a more or less unknown foreign girl came to be presented at the Russian Court and then appointed as a lady-in-waiting to the Czarina, one must understand that Elizabeth was markedly pro-French. By character she was nervous and timid and disliked politics—so much so that when there had been a palace plot to place her on the throne, the ringleaders, including the French Ambassador, had the greatest difficulty in persuading her to agree to it. The Czarina had taken the French Ambassador, Chétardie, as a lover and it was he who, through the Vice-Chancellor, Vorontzoff, introduced Lia to the Court.

While the Vice-Chancellor tended to side with the French, the Chancellor, Bestucheff, was pro-British. For some time he and the British Ambassador, Sir Charles Hanbury-Williams, had worked together for a treaty between Russia and England. Soon Bestucheff found that he was having the greatest difficulty in getting the Czarina to sign the treaty and he mentioned this to the Ambassador. Sir Charles was immediately suspicious of the lovely but mysterious Mlle. Lia and he started to make inquiries about her background. To his dismay, he learned that her supposed uncle, Mackenzie Douglas, had Jacobite connections, a fact which immediately made him suspect. Further inquiries revealed that Douglas was acting under French orders and was probably a spy. Sir Charles reported this to Bestucheff and Douglas was arrested by the Russian police and sent to prison.

Yet in arresting Douglas the pro-British section of the Russian Court overlooked the most influential spy in their midst. For Lia de Beaumont was not a woman at all, but the Chevalier Charles Genèviève Louis Auguste André Timothée d'Eon de Beaumont. Born at Tonnère in France in 1728 of a good family, the Chevalier was by no means a frail, effeminate character, though he had the kind of face which could easily pass for that of an attractive girl. He had proved himself to be an accomplished swordsman and been elected *grand prevôt* of the *Salle d'Armes* as a result. He was brave, resourceful, diplomatic and, after having been admitted to the French bar, had attracted the attention of Louis XV on account of his outstanding intellectual abilities. But no doubt the plan to send him as a spy to the Court of the Czarina was prompted mainly by the knowledge that he could impersonate females to perfection. This talent was said to have been developed because his mother had always dressed him in a girl's clothes from the age of four, a custom which she maintained until he was approaching puberty.

The French knew that the Czarina was surrounded by spies and that any male they sent to St. Petersburg would quickly be suspected. Their one hope was to infiltrate a first class male spy disguised as a female, his assignment being to win the favours of the Czarina and to further the French cause at Court and detach the Russians from the English. This the Chevalier must have accomplished beyond even the most optimistic of French hopes. He seems to have made himself immune from any outside interference at the Russian Court and never to have been suspected even by the Czarina herself. Indeed, it was the Chevalier who eventually revealed his true identity to the Czarina. She is said to have forgiven him for the deception and to have been so impressed with his ability that she offered him a post in her own Government. No doubt Elizabeth hoped to make use of d'Eon as a double-agent. But he declined the offer and in due course returned to Paris, where he was showered with honours and given an annual pension of 3,000 livres by the King.

The Chevalier still lived a dual existence, sometimes serving in the French Army, where he acquired a reputation as brilliant fencer (he was A.D.C. to the Duc de Broglie for a time), and occasionally playing the part of the delectable Mlle. Lia. Then, mainly through the influence of the King, d'Eon was sent on a special mission to London, being given the rank of a Minister Plenipotentiary, though ostesnibly acting as secretary to the French Ambassador. In fact, his real purpose in England was to be a master spy. Once again he was highly successful, intercepting vital documents from the British Foreign Office, obtaining plans from the War Office and personally working out a programme for the best routes for a French army to take, if it should invade England.

Yet d'Eon's fame had made him enemies and among these were some who were jealous of his influence with the King and the fact that in London he was above all a private agent of Louis. He quarrelled with the Count de Guerchy, who had been appointed Ambassador to London, and was ordered to return to France, one of the communications sent to him reminding him how he had served Louis XV "in women's garments" and advising him to put on such attire once again. This was more than a sneer: it was a carefully calculated insult. D'Eon had no intention of going back to Paris to be humiliated in this manner, so he decided to throw himself at the mercy of the English and seek permission to live in London.

Wisely, the British authorities agreed to the Chevalier making his home among them. Perhaps they had their suspicions about his true role in London, as by this time they must have known the true identity of the Czarina's lady-in-waiting. It is possible that d'Eon offered to turn over information to the British and became a double agent. One story is that John Wilkes, the Radical Member of Parliament, who had taken up the Chevalier's cause and was one of his closest friends, recruited him to the British Secret Service. There was, however, never any evidence that he was a traitor to France and Wilkes declared that one reason why d'Eon sought sanctuary in London was because he absolutely refused to revert to his role as a female impersonator.

The truth is that d'Eon was not merely an impostor in the sense that he was a spy who disguised himself as a woman. His impostures went much deeper than that and make him somewhat of a psychological mystery. Indeed, it is a mystery that perhaps will never be completely solved. One knows that he played the role of a woman at the Court of the Czarina, but in both England and France rumours, at first faint, persisted that d'Eon was in fact a woman. There were certain intonations of voice and quirks in his conduct that suggested femininity and it was noted that he not only never married, but avoided having any affairs with women. In the clubs of London wagers were offered on the subject of whether d'Eon was male or female. On May 24th, 1771, a jury of aristocratic ladies examined d'Eon at Medmenham Abbey in Buckinghamshire with the object of delivering a verdict on his true sex. After what they described as "a most thorough investigation" they recorded their opinion that his sex was "doubtful", whatever that might mean. It was a verdict which by no means pleased those who had placed large bets in the hope of obtaining a definite decision one way or another. The controversy concerning d'Eon raged furiously for years and it may well be that the Chevalier delighted in maintaining the charade and keeping people guessing. Various tit-bits of information concerning the Chevalier's past and present were leaked to a public avid for scandal. It was pointed out that, though baptised as a boy, d'Eon had been given the name of Genèviève as well as Charles when he was baptised. It was said that he had been dedicated to the Virgin Mary and offered to the Sisterhood of the Virgin by his mother. It was also rumoured that he had become a member of the strange secret society known as the Hell-Fire Club who held their meetings in caves carved out of the hill beneath the church at West Wycombe.

In 1777 there was a law-suit over the bets placed on the exact sex of the Chevalier. The verdict of "doubtful" was hotly disputed by those who had wagered to the tune of thousands of pounds one way or another on the verdict. The case was heard before Lord Mansfield and it was stated that: "The action was brought by Mr. Hayes, surgeon, against Jacques, a broker and underwriter, for the recovery of seven hundred pounds, Jacques having, about six years before, received premiums of fifteen guineas per cent., for every one of which he stood engaged to return a hundred guineas, whenever it should be proved that the Chevalier d'Eon was actually a woman."

In this cause three witnesses of repute and respectability, two of them members of the medical profession, swore on oath that they had obtained such proof as admitted of no contradiction that d'Eon was a woman. A verdict was then given in favour of the plaintiff, but it was afterwards set aside on a point of law.

Whether d'Eon was amused or humiliated by the result of this trial is not clear. He was, like all good spies, a master of ambivalence and he may well have felt that his ability to masquerade successfully was his trump card whether dealing with the British or the French. From then on he seems to have decided to dress as a woman. What was more surprising was his decision to return to France. Not only had d'Eon personally broken his links with France, but the French had made two attempts to poison him and several attempts to kidnap him from England. The Chevalier had written letters to the English press denouncing his enemies in France and he had raised a private army to protect himself. The French had even gone so far as to engage an English chimney-sweep to hide in the chimney of d'Eon's London house and, by making groaning noises, to cause d'Eon to think the place was haunted. The

Chevalier was not so easily frightened. He guessed what had happened, thrust his sword up the chimney and threatened the chimney-sweep with death if he did not come down and confess who had sent him. D'Eon's revenge for this incident was to publish revelations about the private life of the French king in English newspapers, at the same time letting the sweep go free.

It is not improbable that he returned to France as a double-agent, serving both the British and the French. There is evidence that he kept the British informed on the identities of all French agents in Britain. M. de Vergennes, one of the French Ministers who had originally ordered the Chevalier back to France, stated that it was "the King's will that you should resume the dress of your sex," presumably meaning that of a woman, since d'Eon at that time was clad as a man. When eventually he got back to Paris, this request was repeated in somewhat different terms, in other words he was instructed to remain dressed as a woman. Until his death in 1810 d'Eon complied with this request. Early on in the French Revolution he returned to England after an absence of fourteen years, still dressed as a female. Why he persisted in this charade after leaving France and going back to England, where he had been known as a male, is one of the mysteries of this enigmatic character's life. Perhaps he took a delight in imposture for its own sake, regarding the question of his sex as a matter of complete indifference as far as he was concerned. For, had he any strong feelings either way, he had every opportunity of proving beyond doubt that he was a male even in a country where a trial had ruled that he was a female.

For, when he died, an anatomical examination was carried out by a doctor on the ruling of a Coroner and the doctor stated that d'Eon was "without any shadow of doubt a male person." He was buried as a male at St. Pancras in 1810.

Thus there were three differing verdicts on d'Eon's sex, but it would seem that the last one must be the most acceptable. There was the verdict of the all-female jury that his actual sex was "doubtful", whatever they may have meant by that ambiguous word. The jury under Lord Mansfield seemed quite positive that he was a female, but one wonders whether some of the jury may have been bribed by those who stood to gain vast sums on the result. It is said that more than £100,000 in bets were placed on it. One would like to know the opinion of the Czarina Elizabeth. She had the reputation of being a devourer of men at all times of the day and night, and lackeys, choirboys and coachmen were among her lovers. When d'Eon confessed his true sex to her, did she personally confirm this?

An eighteenth century imposter of a totally different order was Giuseppe Balsamo, the son of a peasant family of Palermo, born in 1743, but who is probably better known as Count Cagliostro.

There have been attempts to deny that Balsamo and Cagliostro were one and the same person. Casanova is said to have declared that, though he met Balsamo, he never encountered Cagliostro. Nevertheless, all the evidence would seem to point to Cagliostro being an alias for Balsamo.

He has been variously described as "the great liar", one of the biggest scoundrels who ever lived and "an eighteenth century Rasputin;" yet all these verdicts fail to take account of the fact that Cagliostro possessed certain remarkable talents and was one of the most fascinating figures of all time. The historian, Thomas Carlyle, called him the "King of Liars", but in the latter part of this twentieth century it is gradually being realised that he was an extraordinary occultist.

As a youth he was enrolled as a novice at a monastery, but was thrown out for blasphemy. Most likely he deliberately behaved in such a manner that he would be automatically expelled. Then he took lessons in art and showed sufficient talent to make a living by doing design work. About this time he seems to have discovered that he possessed telepathic faculties, or what would then be called second sight. During the daytime Balsamo, as he was then known, worked hard at his drawing and painting, but at night spent his time consorting with the underworld, learning their tricks and seeking to copy them. Not surprisingly, he landed up in jail.

When he came out of prison, Balsamo set about learning to become a competent forger. He put this new talent to the test within his own family circle. Having learned to make perfect copies of his sister's handwriting, he forged a letter to her lover, indicating that she would like to have a necklace and some other trinkets. His trick succeeded and he was able to intercept the presents when they arrived and to send back a forged "thank you" note. Nor was the forgery discovered until some years later.

Balsamo was as versatile as he was resourceful. He next turned his attention to the occult and, as with everything else he took up, he studied this in great detail. Thus he began to understand his own remarkable gift for telepathy and worked hard to develop this for money-making purposes. In Palermo he took good care that news of his clairvoyant activities should be circulated far and wide. Having made sure that a goldsmith named Marano should be one of those to be told of Balsamo's second sight, he told this man, under a pledge of the utmost secrecy, that treasure was buried in a cave some distance outside Palermo. Marano must have been as gullible as he was greedy, for he seems to have failed to inquire why Balsamo had not himself taken the treasure when, for a modest sum in gold, he offered to show the other man where it was buried. The money was handed over and the pair set off for the cave where the goldsmith was told exactly where he had to dig. Previously Balsamo had warned Marano that the cave and its treasure were guarded by a host of demons. While Marano was digging, a bunch of ruffians, posing as demons, specially hired by Balsamo, rushed out of the depths of the cave and knocked the goldsmith senseless. When Marano came to, Balsamo told him that the demons had made off with the treasure. Days later Marano, who had complained to the police, began to realise that he had been robbed and made to look a fool. He vowed to kill Balsamo, but that young man promptly disappeared from Palermo.

That is the true story about the early life of Balsamo. But in his autobiography Count Cagliostro told a much more colourful and romantic story. According to his own account, he was the son of a Maltese nobleman, who was orphaned at the age of three months, taken to Medina in Arabia and educated by "the chief of the Mahomeddan religion". Then he described how he was taught most of the "oriental languages" and given a secret insight into "the pyramids of Egypt, those repositories of human knowledge, sheltering the precious trust from the injuries of time." Afterwards he travelled to Egypt, Africa and Asia, was chosen to be a "secret agent of the Church of Christ" among the infidels and that for this mission he was made one of the Knights of Malta. Later in Rome he was received several times in audience by the Pope and became the friend of Cardinals.

Amidst all these fantasies which Cagliostro (or Balsamo) chose to weave into his autobiography one undisputed fact stands out: "in my twenty-second year . . . I met a young lady of quality, Signorina Serafina Feliciani, whose exquisite charms caused a flame of passion to burn within me, a flame which many years of marriage has never faltered."

This story is true except for the minor detail that the girl's real name was Lorenza, not Serafina, the latter title undoubtedly being inspired by the fact that the seraphim, or choir of angels, were supposed to be specially distinguished in ancient mythology for their ardent passions. Lorenza was fifteen years old when Balsamo met her and, though of humble birth, she possessed quality in the shape of her delicately chiselled features and her undoubted beauty. Soon she was to become an apt pupil in the arts of imposture under the guidance of her husband. They went to Rome after living in Campo, the home town of Lorenza, and here they practised forgery on a considerable scale. As the police began to close in on them, so they moved on elsewhere, to Milan, Genoa and on into France. On several occasions the pair posed as pilgrims, travelling from one shrine to another across Italy and begging as they went, Lorenza supplementing this by prostitution and blackmail. But when these tactics were tried out in Spain the couple met their match. The ruse had always been that Lorenza would make an assignment with some wealthy man and then her husband would rush into the room when she screamed, demanding compensation. But the Viceroy of Catalonia not only refused to pay up, but ordered them both to leave the district.

On his first visit to London Balsamo had little luck and left as poor as when he arrived. Travelling on to Paris, he decided that skilful imposture was more lucrative than petty crime and he turned his attention to offering elixirs to long life, love potions and beauty ointments to a gullible public. He was goaded into doing this through the unfaithfulness of his wife. For whereas she had been quite content to go out prostituting herself for both their sakes while remaining with Balsamo, eventually she had grown weary of this one-sided arrangement, which had never taken them much higher than a bare existence, and ran off with a wealthy man.

Balsamo was so angry at what he regarded as her treachery that he appealed to the Courts to deal with his erring wife. He won his case and Lorenza was imprisoned in the women's penitentiary. When she was released, it was a demure and subservient wife who returned to her husband and promised never again to leave him. Meanwhile Balsamo had done so well out of his elixir trade that their fortunes changed sufficiently for them to be able to travel around in their own coach.

Sometime later it was "Count Allesandro Cagliostro" who turned up in London with the "Countess Serafina". This part of the autobiography is true. It seemed as though as soon as he assumed the role of the mysterious Count with his Arabic and oriental associations, Balsamo acquired a sureness of touch and a will to succeed such as he had never possessed before in his vagabond career. Setting up a laboratory for the manufacture of his elixirs, love potions and ointments, Cagliostro (as he was now known in the capital) made his first real bid for power and influence. This time there was no going back to the petty crime and pimping of his Italian days. Instead of using Lorenza as a bait for wealthy and amorous old men, he told people that the "Countess Serafina" was approaching seventy years of age and that she owed her astonishingly youthful looks to an elixir which he made himself and which he called "the Wine of Egypt".

There was, of course, no rejuvenating property in this so-called elixir, but if it did not actually make the old look younger, or preserve the looks of those approaching middle-age, it enabled them to have an appetite for sexual adventures. For the elixir which Balsamo and Lorenza concocted together contained cantharides, that stimulant to the genito-urinary organs which is better known as Spanish Fly. Like Edward Kelley before him, Cagliostro also claimed to be searching for the secrets of turning base metals into gold. He was quite certain that he would very soon be successful in this quest, he told people, because he had the gift of second sight and an ancient manuscript to guide him. Another of his claims was that this ancient manuscript could, if consulted, provide winning numbers for lottery games.

Unfortunately there were others who were so gullible that they really believed that Cagliostro's ancient manuscript must contain the key to vast riches and they plotted to relieve him of it. The plot involved having Cagliostro arrested on a bogus charge and then breaking into his rooms and stealing his manuscript. But when they obtained it, they found to their dismay that they could not understand a single word of it and were forced to ask Cagliostro to reveal its secrets. The "Count", who had by now been released from prison, laughed in their faces. But the plotters were persistent: they brought another charge against Cagliostro, having discovered someone who had lent the bogus Count money which he had never repaid. Before he could regain his freedom, Cagliostro had to pay out considerable sums of money.

His second visit to England looked like ending in disaster as did his first, but in the long term he gained certain advantages. In the first place he had managed while in London to be admitted into the Esperance Lodge of Freemasons, an organisation which was then far more concerned with the occult, alchemists and astrologers than it is today. What it offered was not merely a kind of alternative religion, but the sense of belonging to the most ancient religion in the world and one which guarded ancient occult secrets.

Up to now Cagliostro's own particular brand of conmanship had not shown itself to be on a high level. But from the time he became a Mason there was a great metamorphosis both in his character and his tactics. Colin Wilson, in his book *The Occult*, wrote that up to that moment Cagliostro "had remained an adventurer on much the same level as Casanova, an artist driven from pillar to post by adversity", but that with his becoming a Freemason "the transformation was total . . .

From then on freemasonry was his life's work."

What Cagliostro did was to use his mysterious ancient manuscripts (he acquired others while he was in London) to build up his own species of Freemasonry. He claimed that as a result of consulting the ancient manuscripts he had been given second sight to learn the secrets of the pyramids and those of the ancient prophets, Elijah and Enoch. Of course this was in part the beginning of a new series of confidence tricks, but there was more to it than that. It was as though a petty thief had suddenly acquired the status of a Messiah, or a travelling illusionist had developed genuine powers of extra-sensory perception. The second sight with which he had long been credited blossomed into an astonishing talent for clairvoyance, using young children as mediums.

This talent was naturally all important in Cagliostro's other aim of spreading the doctrine of Freemasonry, or, as he called it, to distinguish it from the orthodox Freemasonry, Egyptian Freemasonry. He laid down his own doctrines for this cult, producing his own Order Book, which, suggest some of his biographers, may have been written by someone else as there are doubts whether Cagliostro himself was ever truly literate. Women as well as men were permitted to join the Order, of which he assumed the title of Grand Master, bestowing the rank of Grand Mistress on his wife. Scrying by means of gazing into bowls of water was a feature of some of the ceremonies of his cult.

Thus Cagliostro set out on a tour of Europe, establishing Masonic Lodges wherever he went—Berlin, Leipzig, Nuremberg, and Venice. By the 1780's he had become a rich man, travelling in a lacquered coach, on which were painted his magic symbols, and having six liveried servants. Yet, curiously, he was relatively frugal in his style of living. He made a point of staying in a poor quarter of whatever city he visited and actually gave away considerable sums to the needy. Meanwhile, there are many independently vouched for examples of his talent for clairvoyance. He seemed to be able not only to detect illness, or the approach of illness, but in some cases to prescribe cures. People flocked to him with their troubles. He cured the Marquis de Lasalle of a gangrenous leg. He sold his bogus rejuvenation potions again in St. Petersburg because he failed to set up a Masonic Lodge in the Russian capital, though the Empress Catherine was fascinated by him and impressed by his healing sessions. Eventually, Cagliostro's fame spread to Paris where Cardinal Rohan, who was interested in alchemy, expressed a desire to see him.

Cagliostro then went to Paris where both he and Lorenza won the confidence of the Cardinal, so much so, in fact, that Rohan said of Cagliostro that the knowledge of "this most extraordinary, most sublime man" was "equalled only by his goodness". The Cardinal had a cousin, the Prince de Soubise, who was said by his doctors to be fast approaching death, though they were unable to diagnose his illness. Cagliostro was consulted, he made a certain prescription and declared that if the Prince took this, he would soon be fully recovered in health. Events swiftly proved Cagliostro to be right once more.

After this the reputation of the "Count" and his wife was enormously enhanced, for Rohan was full of gratitude for the saving of Soubise's life. But it was this very friendship with Rohan which once again brought sudden disaster into the life of Cagliostro. The Cardinal had acquired an attractive young mistress in the person of the Countess de la Motte who had become a confidante of Queen Marie Antoinette. Rohan had not been on good terms with the Queen for some time and he thought he could use the influence of his mistress to work towards a better relationship with Marie Antoinette. He pleaded with the Countess to do all she could to forward his cause with the Queen. But the

Countess, while falling in with this plan, saw what she believed was a short cut to riches. She knew that the Queen desperately wanted a diamond necklace which had been made by two Parisian jewellers, but that the price was too high—the equivalent of some 400,000 dollars. So, believing that Rohan was wealthy, the Countess asked him to buy the necklace secretly for the Queen. The Cardinal fell in with the plan with incredible naivety, obtaining the necklace on credit, and being convinced by letters which had been cleverly forged that the Queen had forgiven him and that he was received back into the royal favour. The Countess even arranged for a courtesan to put on a wig and pose as the Queen for a nocturnal meeting with Rohan, who went to his assignment disguised as a musketeer. Even then he had no suspicions of a plot against him and seems to have been content just to be allowed to kiss the "royal" foot.

The Countess, with her impoverished husband, then collected the necklace and set about selling off the diamonds one by one. Rohan realised what had happened and then failed to pay the first instalment when it was due, for, contrary to general belief, he was not a rich man. Scandal inevitably broke over the heads of the participants. The Cardinal was sent to the Bastille along with the Countess and the woman who had impersonated the Queen as well as the forger of the letters.

Cagliostro was innocent of any knowledge of the plot, but he had allowed himself to be unconsciously involved by the plotters. The Cardinal had told him about the purchase of the necklace and the other plotters sought to direct attention away from themselves by trying to incriminate Cagliostro with the police. They claimed that the Count had conjured up visions of how the Cardinal could placate the Queen when scrying in a bowl of water.

Cagliostro and his wife were arrested and tried in the spring of 1786. They were able to prove that they were out of Paris when the necklace was actually bought and, when acquitted, a large crowd gathered to cheer them back to their apartments. All the same the pair were ordered to leave France. They returned to England for a while, then went on to Switzerland where another Egyptian Masonic Lodge was established. Then he made the fatal mistake—against his own instinctive judgement, it is said—of returning to Italy. Lorenza had expressed a wish to see her parents once more.

Thus in May, 1789, the couple turned up in Rome. It was the very chance for which the secret agents of the Vatican were waiting. Cagliostro's missionary work for Freemasonry had long been noted at the Vatican and it had been decided that he was a dangerous enemy of the Catholic Church.

He was arrested on charges of sorcery and propagating Freemasonry, and the Papal police had no difficulty in finding witnesses to testify against him and insist that he practised black magic. To humiliate him still further, Cagliostro was charged under his real name of Balsamo. Sentenced to a long term of imprisonment, he was held first at San Angelo and then at San Leone, where he was confined in a windowless cellar without light or sanitation, food being let down to him through a trap-door in the ceiling.

When the French invaded the Papal States and the fortress of San Leone in 1795, the fate of Cagliostro was one of the first matters they inquired into. They were told that he had died a few days previously.

But had he? Or did Cagliostro have the last laugh and hoax his tormentors? His books and manuscripts were burned by order of the Papal Inquisition. His wife was sent to life imprisonment at a penitentiary for women in Rome. The great con-trickster himself was a broken man. Yet some writers suggest that he was always thinking up ways and means of escaping and that his guards were always on the alert in case he hoodwinked them. The Cagliostro magic was still capable of alarming even his captors.

One story is that Cagliostro escaped from his prison and took refuge in Russia where, for a while, he lived in the home of Madame Blavatsky's father. It is said that "in the midst of winter he produced by magical power a plate full of fresh strawberries for a sick person who was craving for it". Madame Blavatsky became the founder of the Theosophical Movement and was herself an authority on the occult. Did she learn all this from her father who obtained instruction from Cagliostro?

Most probably he died in jail, but no proof of his death or of how he died has ever been provided. In 1795 he would have been fifty-two, not too old to have made an escape and certainly still shrewd and cunning enough to trick his guards. One cannot help hoping that this likeable rascal pulled off just one last trick.

6

LADY HAMILTON'S CELESTIAL BED

PERHAPS THE "Celestial Bed" would never have been remembered but for the fact that biographers delving into the life of Admiral Nelson's mistress, Lady Hamilton, discovered her association with it.

Lady Hamilton, the wife of Sir William Hamilton, British Ambassador at Naples, was born Emma Lyon, a native of Cheshire. At an early age she went to London and, while still in her late teens, was engaged in somewhat dubious activities in a notorious establishment called "The Temple of Health", which was set up in London in 1780. It is not clear whether the Temple had two branches, or whether it moved from one address to another, but it was conducted both in the Adelphi and in Pall Mall. In 1780 Emma Lyon would have been at the zenith of her beauty and it was probably about this time that Romney was attracted to her and made the first of his many portraits of this great Georgian charmer.

Emma was said to have been the "Hostess of the Celestial Bed", though she was actually described simply as "a Goddess of Health, who sang soothing melodies to patients."

The bed itself was the invention of a talented confidence trickster, with an inventive turn of mind, who called himself "Dr. Graham". Nobody seems to have discovered what his first name was, or even if "Graham" was his real name. Rumour had it that he came from Scotland and was quite well connected, but whether he had ever qualified as a doctor is doubtful. But he arrived in London at a time when the idle rich were eagerly looking for novel recreations and a *nouveau frisson* to prevent them from being bored. The "Temple of Health" provided this.

"Dr. Graham" took good care to advertise his establishment, having footmen dressed in livery with gold-laced hats standing outside the doors, handing out pamphlets to passers-by. Once they were enticed in they could not fail to be impressed by the opulence and magnificence of the interior. Graham cleverly combined an atmosphere of eroticism and luxury with some of the outward symbols of a health clinic. His salesmanship was particularly subtle: summed up, his message was "indulge yourself as much as you like here and it will benefit and not harm your health". It was a message that was particularly welcome to the jaded, gouty and near-impotent old men who tottered up the steps not quite knowing whether they wanted a cure, or an afternoon or evening's lechery.

The salons of the Temple had stained-glass windows and were filled with marble statues and "satin sofas on glass legs". The setting up of the establishment must have cost a small fortune and to recover his money and make a substantial profit Graham needed to be able to charge high fees. He seems to have achieved this by offering a wide range of "cures", "administrations to Personal Delectation", "earth baths", "Divine Balm" and, of course, the Celestial Bed. Nearly all these "wares" were fraudulent and based on sheer quackery, but Graham gave them the semblance of respectability and orthodoxy and seems to have convinced many that he really was a doctor. He eschewed black magic, or any similar mumbo-jumbo, made no pretensions as a faith healer, as, by going all out for the educated and wealthy, he needed to sound and seem something more than a quack.

Graham sold a *Treatise on Health*, written by himself, at half a guinea a copy and this set out his theories and the goods and delights he had to offer. Like Balsamo before him, he offered an "elixir of life", which was more an aphrodisiac than a rejuvenator, but he made no extravagant claims for it, no suggestion that it was based on ancient Egyptian prescriptions. In 1775 Alessandro, Count Volta, the Italian physicist, invented the electrophore and shortly afterwards constructed the earliest absolute electrometer and the electric pile, the latter of which he first described in a letter to the Royal Society of London. Perhaps Graham had met the Count, or at least had heard of his inventions, but he claimed to have the first "electric machine" in the whole of London.

While one might be censorious of some of Graham's quackery and bogus cures, it is possible that he was far-sighted in his attempts to use the "electrical machine" as part of a health cure. He charged vast sums for this electrical treatment "for those Long Suffering Gentlemen who have been attacked by the Scourge of Rheumatism and Gout", but it is said that some of the wealthy cripples who hobbled up his steps actually benefited from the treatment. But Graham made no attempt to share his theories and secrets of the "electrical machine" either with other medicos or anyone else outside his Temple.

But the *pièce de résistance* of the Temple of Health was the "Celestial Bed." Contemporary accounts of this bed vary considerably, probably depending on the sobriety or otherwise of those who actually sampled its delights, but all are agreed that it was magnificent and impressive. One man about town of the era, who wrote under the *nom de plume* of "Trojan", gives this detailed account of the bed and also throws a little light on Graham himself:

"Quite the most sensational of all the recuperative properties in the Temple of Health is the Celestial Bed, or perhaps the Electro-Magnetic Bed might be a more appropriate designation. It is the creation of that most ingenious of medicos, the good Doctor James Graham, who is said to come from Cowgate, Edinburgh, where he was born in the year of the Great Rebellion of 1745.

"The doctor lectures on the various uses of his bed and his beautiful assistant is a young girl named Emma Lyon, who is described by the aforesaid doctor as the Perfect Example of Health and Beauty to be found in London. A Goddess of Health he calls her, and indeed to look at her is as good a tonic as a glass of champagne.

"I would compare the Celestial Bed to that Celebrated Bed of Ware, though it is not so large, but in due course may become even more famous. To spend a single night in the bed costs as much as one hundred pounds, but there are other electric-magnetic beds for which the charge is only half as much. The doctor says that he has spent some sixty thousand [pounds, presumably] on the construction of the Celestial Bed and that if any woman sleeps in it she is guaranteed to have a beautiful child."

Timbs in his *Doctors and Patients* also describes the "Celestial Bed" and what he calls a "Magnetic Throne" and it is he who first recorded the early pranks of Emma, Lady Hamilton, in what must have been a barely disguised high-class bordello.

What is not clear from the somewhat ambiguous accounts of the Temple of Health is whether Graham supplied the females who were to produce the beautiful children, or if the male clients brought the prospective mothers with them. Perhaps the "doctor" obliged when requested. It would be fascinating to know whether the voluptuous Emma was one of those who so "obliged". Yet it may well be that the Temple of Health provided Emma with the knowledge and background which made her find favour later on with Nelson himself. For one commentator on the Temple of Health stated that the chief clients were "captains of privateers, nabobs, spendthrifts and old noblemen." From the first-named no doubt Emma learned a great deal about the tastes and foibles of sea captains and the subjects they liked to talk about.

It would also be interesting to know if Graham had any female clients and, if so, whether they went to sample the Celestial Bed in quest of beautiful children. His favourite clients seem to have been those who had health worries—the rheumatics and arthritics, the impotent and those worried about whether they could produce an heir, and the very many whose feverish lives and dissolute habits had made them prematurely aged. First, these clients were lured into taking "earth baths" and given "divine massage" (nobody explains how this was given, whether by human or mechanical means) and after this treatment, rather on the same lines as a modern hydro establishment, they were introduced to the delights of the "electro-magnetic beds". For these smaller and less dramatised beds a fee of fifty pounds a session was charged. The object of these beds was not to provide a sleeping partner, but to ensure a sound sleep and treatment which would be "conducive to restoring the natural vigour and virility of the human body"; in other words, the promise of getting the clients ship-shape for further amatory conquests.

Presumably the more gullible clients, those with more money than sense and those for whom the other "cures" had little effect, were ultimately persuaded to pay up one hundred pounds for the pleasure, honour, call it what you will, of sleeping in the "Celestial Bed"; Graham created the illusion of conferring an honour on his clients when he put this bed at their disposal, describing it as his "Holy of Holies", "the Throne of Supreme Grace" and the "Penultimate Pleasure". The bed itself was supported by six solid glass legs and its drapings and sheets, its pillows and other accessories were doused in a perfume of reputedly aphrodisiac properties, "guaranteed to arouse in anyone the most dormant feelings of passion and the most fervent sentiments". In addition there was the electricity sending little shocks and shivers through the mattress and a "self-playing organ" which may also have been operated by electricity, though there is no description of how this functioned. One can only suppose that the intention was to lull clients to sleep while Emma Lyon sang to the music.

It would seem as though James Graham, if indeed James was his name, got away with his impostures without being prosecuted. There is no record of any court case concerning him. But probably his clients became impatient because his "cures" did not work, except for the lucky few who were able to convince themselves that they were efficacious, a psychological factor upon which Graham undoubtedly relied for his success. That business at the Temple of Health must have declined seems to be borne out by the fact that eventually all its trappings, including the "Celestial Bed", were sold at a public auction. Graham himself died in 1794.

The case of Kaspar Hauser is perhaps one of the most curious confidence tricks of all time, unique in that in this instance nobody can be sure who the con-trickster was. Lord Stanhope, the British statesman who took an interest in the case, eventually decided that Hauser himself was an imposter. But he brought forward no proof and, in the final analysis, the identity of the trickster is pure guess-work and there may well have been two tricksters competing with one another. Nevertheless, such an unusual story is worth telling even if it ends inconclusively in mystery.

In December, 1833, a young man died in hospital at Ansbach in Bavaria following stab wounds received some days ealier. His name was Kaspar Hauser, but nobody knew where he came from and his murderer was never discovered. He was buried in a local church graveyard and a tombstone was eventually erected there, carrying this inscription in Latin:

"Here lies Kaspar Hauser, Enigma of his Times. His parentage is unknown, his death a mystery. XIV Dec. MDCCCXXXIII."

And in the royal park marking the site of his murder is a small granite column on which is this blunt and somewhat ambiguous text in Latin:

"Here an unknown has been killed by an unknown, XIV DEC. MDCCCXXXIII."

There is in this text a suspicion that whoever authorised it thought there was a hint of suicide rather than murder.

For years these stones attracted not only the curious and morbid, but many amateur detectives who were anxious to solve the mystery of Kaspar. His story aroused interest in many countries and was a subject of gossip throughout the various German empires and grand duchies. In some countries bordering on Germany it was whispered that the murder was the result of a dastardly plot in high society.

Kaspar first appeared in Nuremberg on May 28th, 1828. Before that date there was absolutely no record of him anywhere. It was a public holiday and the streets were more or less deserted when a shoemaker noticed a youth of about fifteen wandering aimlessly along the streets. He was wearing tattered old clothes and seemed to be poorly nourished with his pinched face and thin body.

But for his blonde hair and blue eyes the boy might have been taken for a wandering gypsy, but there was a certain peculiar air of distinction about him which attracted the shoemaker's attention. As he paused to glance at the youth, the latter thrust an envelope into his hands. It was addressed to the Officer-in-charge of

Recruiting, Nuremberg.

The shoemaker spoke to the boy, asking him who had written the letter, but received no reply. He shrugged his shoulders and conducted the boy to the local Recruiting Office, pointing to the door and indicating that he should knock. The boy nodded and the shoemaker left him.

Later the Recruiting Officer told his part of the story: "I was not in when the lad called at my office and my servant told him to wait. The boy seemed ravenously hungry and thirsty, so he was given some water and food. Then he lay down on the floor and went to sleep. This is where he was when I found him.

"He gave me the envelope and inside were the most meagre details provided anonymously. The writer stated that he had been looking after the lad since he was a baby, that his father had been an officer in a cavalry regiment, but was now dead. The lad, whose name was Kaspar, wished more than anything else to become a soldier like his father. The only other information was that the boy was born on April 30th, 1812, but there was no indication of his surname.

"I thought the whole affair was distinctly odd. I questioned the boy closely, but got very little more out of him. When I asked him who he was and where he had come from, he just replied that he did not know. But he kept repeating that he wished to be a soldier like his father. I found it hard to make up my mind as to whether the boy was an imbecile, or whether he had been told to behave in this manner. I didn't want him for a recruit and I suspected something mysterious was going on, so I handed him over to the police.

The police stripped the boy and all they found on him were a handkerchief bearing the initials "KH" and a rosary. But still the boy insisted he "didn't know" anything. Thinking that a taste of prison would make him talk, they locked him up in a cell. But as the days passed Kaspar still declined to talk and did not seem to mind being confined to a cell. They noticed that while he ate bread and drank water eagerly enough, he did not seem to care for any other food.

News of the mystery boy travelled fast. The Nuremberg City authorities offered a reward to anyone who could provide information concerning him, but nobody came forward. The townspeople began to be sympathetic towards the young prisoner and there was an agitation for him to be released. This was done and, given the surname of Hauser because of the second initial on the handkerchief, Kaspar was sent to live under the protection of a Professor Daumer, who had shown a special interest in him.

Eventually Daumer taught Kaspar how to read and write and then persuaded him to write down the story of his life. What he told was an astonishing narrative. "For longer than I can remember—certainly for many years—I have been kept locked up in a small, dark room. It was very dark all the time because there were shutters over the window. I never had any lighting. When my food was brought to me I could never see who brought it because he never carried a light. I was given only bread and water. I saw nothing of the outside world at any time; I was taught nothing."

It was an astonishing, almost an unbelievable story, and Professor Daumer suggested that independent scholars might interview Kaspar and see if they could deduce or learn anything more about his origins. The police, who at first had been inclined to think that Kaspar was an idiot who had escaped from an asylum, now began to think there might be something more sinister behind the whole strange affair. One theory was that the boy had been planted in Nuremberg as a spy, the aim being to have him recruited into the Army. Others thought his story might just be true and that someone in high society had kept him prisoner for years.

But to all these theories there was no rational answer.

Kaspar never changed his story under any amount of cross-examination. He continued to behave like someone who has been locked up all his life and, though growing up fast and developing physically, he behaved like a boy and enjoyed playing with toys. On the other hand, he did not appear to be sub-normal and doctors who examined him could find no defects.

The mystery deepened when in October, 1829, came the first of three attempts on Kaspar's life. He was found unconscious with a wound on his head. When asked what had happened, the youth said that he had been attacked by "a man with a black face". But he had no idea who his assailant was.

Police took the view that the attacker was probably wearing a black mask over his face, as there was no information about any negro in the area. It was then that the theory was developed that Kaspar must have run away from captivity and that his captors had found out where he was and wanted him out of the way.

This theory was further strengthened when, several weeks later, Kaspar was found with a bullet wound in his head. It was not a serious wound and he soon recovered, but when questioned by the police—this time in much greater detail—Kaspar told a surprising story. He said that he had found the pistol lying on the floor of his room, that he had picked it up and that "it went off accidentally".

This story seemed unlikely and some people began to suspect that Kaspar was a liar, or mentally unstable. However, there seemed to be no disputing that there had been one attack on the youth. The question now was whether somebody had slipped into Kaspar's room and deliberately placed a loaded pistol there in the hope that he would pick it up and accidentally shoot himself. Another possibility was that Kaspar was in some strange way the central figure in an imposture or a hoax.

Surgeons began to study his case. In some ways his mental state seemed to bear out the kind of experiences he had in the past. He wrote of himself: "I knew nothing of the world so long as I was shut up . . . I have had two wooden horses and a dog and with these I have always played . . . The prison in which I was obliged to live until my release was, perhaps, six or seven feet long, four broad and five high . . . On the ground was laid some straw on which I used to eat and sleep." Yet one or two doctors took the view that Kaspar was so quick to learn that it seemed improbable that he could have been shut up in such conditions for so long.

It was about this time that Lord Stanhope arrived in Nuremberg and heard the story of Kaspar when dining out with friends. He immediately asked to be introduced to the youth, for the Under-Secretary of State for Foreign Affairs had a passion for detective work and for delving into mysteries. He mainly satisfied this yearning by becoming an historian and it was said that, through this talent for ferreting around in unsuspected places he had access to private documents which were inaccessible to other writers. So he, too, questioned Kaspar and decided to offer to take the boy on a tour of some of the neighbouring cities. He was impressed by the manner in which Kaspar, despite the story of his upbringing, had managed to learn to read and write and behave normally and intelligently at last.

Previously Kaspar had been a charge on the community of Nuremberg and when Lord Stanhope accepted financial responsibility for him, none of the citizens of the Bavarian city demurred. Yet one cannot help wondering whether Lord Stanhope had other motives for the interest he took in Kaspar besides mere curiosity. Did he believe that Kaspar might be the unwanted son of some noble family? Had he been asked to inquire into the mystery by some of his continental friends? Was there an ulterior motive behind his seeming generosity? For

Stanhope spent considerable sums of money on Kaspar, engaging an ex-soldier to protect him, paying for his board and lodging and even employing a detective to investigate the case.

It seemed to many in Bavaria that there was more to it than mere altruism on Stanhope's part and this belief was accentuated when the British statesman suddenly turned against the boy and denounced him as "this miserable impostor". This was a surprising turn-about for only just before he made this statement, Stanhope had arranged for Kaspar to make his future home in England. Some suspected that Stanhope's motives were sinister and when he suddenly announced that he had changed his mind about Kaspar there was a good deal of antagonism to the Earl in Ansbach.

A strange story was told about Stanhope and Kaspar just before the Earl left for England. Stanhope asked Kaspar to show him his diary, but the young man declined to do this, insisting that it was private. Stanhope then asked two of his assistants to search Kaspar's room for the diary when the boy was out of the house. It was never learned whether the diary was found by Stanhope, but certainly there was no trace of the book after Kaspar's death.

Kaspar had been found a post as a clerk in Ansbach and it was here that on December 14th, 1838, the third and fatal attack on him took place. With blood pouring from a wound in his chest, Kaspar returned to his lodgings that day, begging for aid. His story was that he had been told by a complete stranger that a friend of his wanted to see him in the town park. Kaspar obeyed the stranger's instructions and waited on a park bench until another unknown person came along and stabbed him.

A few days later Kaspar died from his wounds. The police never found his killer.

Who in this strange story was the confidence trickster? Was it somebody who had kept Kaspar a prisoner for years, or could it have been Kaspar himself? Some in Ansbach, strongly supported by Lord Stanhope, insisted that Kaspar himself was the impostor and that the alleged attacks on him were invented by Kaspar and the wounds were self-inflicted. Lord Stanhope took the view that the truth about the incident in the park was that Kaspar had stabbed himself, that in effect he had committed suicide to draw attention to himself.

But others took a different view. Lady Caroline Albersdorf said that Stanhope was Kaspar's murderer and others testified that Stanhope had been seen in the vicinity of the park about the time of the alleged attack. Certainy it was established that he had returned to Ansbach the day before. One theory was that Kaspar, tired of carrying on his imposture and dreading his final exposure, had decided to make a hero of himself with the story of yet another attack on him.

Or was Kaspar knowingly part of a cunning imposture practised for some mysterious reason only to find himself liquidated when there appeared to be a danger that somebody might discover the truth about the boy? There is much about Kaspar's story that simply does not ring true. Stanhope himself is said to have believed that the boy might have come from noble stock, or at least he did until he so inexplicably turned against Kaspar. One story put forward years later was that Kaspar was really the son of Charles, the Grand Duke of Baden, and that there was a plot to smuggle him away and keep him in imprisonment until he was grown up. But, owing either to lack of funds or sheer indifference, the people responsible for looking after the child decided to release him in Nuremberg and hoped he would be allowed to join the Army. When they saw how their plan had misfired, either they or the original plotters decided to kill Kaspar. But this so-called explanation of Kaspar's origins is no more credible than Kaspar's own story. Yet it seems to have impressed Kaiser Wilhelm I sufficiently for him to ask the German newspapers in 1875 to print the fact that the prince of the House of Baden had in fact died as a baby in 1812, underlining this with testimonies from no fewer than six doctors. For the Kaiser's daughter was at this time about to marry the Grand Duke of Baden of that era.

But in all this speculation there is more than a possibility that malicious-minded people close to the court of Baden seized on the identity of Kaspar Hauser as someone around whom they could build the legend of a missing German prince. We may never know the truth now as most of the papers on this case have long since disappeared. The documents relating to the inquiry into the death of Hauser disappeared as long ago as 1835 and most of the other papers were destroyed in aerial bombardment in World War II.

7

TRICKSTERS OF THE ART WORLD

OF ALL the arts that of painting is perhaps the most easy for talented impostors to exploit and so it has been down the ages, dating back to the time when Juan de Pereja, the mulatto slave of the great artist, Velasquez, deceived King Philip IV of Spain.

Juan was employed to mix the colours for Velasquez and he soon found he had a real talent for painting. As a slave, however, he was banned from being allowed to practice the art. Juan found that his ambition and the knowledge of how skilled he was at copying his master's work caused him to risk the royal displeasure and even that of Velasquez. He decided that his best course was to made known his talents to the King himself. One of his tasks, when the King came to see Velasquez's work, was to turn round each picture and hold it up for the royal inspection. So Juan, having taken great pains to copy one of his master's pictures, substituted this for Velasquez's own work and presented it to the King. When Philip praised the picture the slave fell on his knees and confessed what he had done, begging forgiveness.

The King turned to Velasquez and commented: "It is indeed a magnificent picture, well worthy of yourself, Velasquez. You must overlook this offence and note that talents such as your slave's warrant that he should be emancipated".

This was, perhaps, one of the most honourable examples of imposture in the sphere of painting and it had a happy ending, for Juan de Pereja was not only freed from slavery, but permitted to go on working for Velasquez.

Nicholas Laniere, an Italian painter of the seventeenth century, was one of the earliest of the skilled tricksters in this field. He passed off copies for originals of work by great masters, tempering his colours with soot and then, rolling his works up, he made them crackle and contract as though they were ancient canvasses. The same antique appearance has been achieved by modern copyists by using a dark varnish on new pictures and then baking them in a slow oven.

Behind the statue of King Charles I at Charing Cross lies a story of remarkable resourcefulness by a confidence trickster of Stuart times. The statue was the work of Le Soeur, a Huguenot sculptor who arrived in England in 1628, and in 1633 this sculpture of the King on horseback was placed on a plot of ground in King Street, Covent Garden. In 1642, on the outbreak of the Civil War, the statue was hidden in the crypt of a church nearby. Eight years later the Cromwellian authorities acting through the Council of State, ordered a search to be made for the work.

When eventually the statue was found it was seized by the Cromwellians and sold "for the rate of old brass, by the pound rate" to one John Rivett, a brazier who lived at the Dial near Holborn Conduit. Rivett was instructed to break up the statue and ensure that it was totally destroyed. Despite the fact that his orders implied that imprisonment or death might be meted out to him if he disobeyed, Rivett showed remarkable aplomb and ingenuity. Perhaps his aesthetic sense would not permit him to destroy the statue, or, more likely, he believed that in time the Cromwellians would be removed and the monarchy restored. At any rate he dug a large and long grave in his garden in Holborn and deposited the statue therein, burying it unspoiled. At the same time, to prove to his masters that he had carried out their wishes, he made and sold "knife-handles, candlesticks, nut-crackers, bodkins, thimbles, spoons and patty-pans" which he claimed he had created from the material of the statue. He took great care to use the exact materials from which the statue had been carved.

What is more, Rivett found no difficulty in selling these articles at high prices to both Cromwellians and Royalists. The former were glad to buy practical evidence that Rivett had broken up the statue of the hated King, while the Royalists were only to anxious to possess souvenirs of their martyred monarch. But there may have been another reason for Rivett's imposture on all and sundry. He, like Le Soeur, was of Huguenot descent and he may have been protecting the sculptor's work. After the Restoration the statue was eventually produced undamaged and Andrew Marvell described how in 1675 "for more pageantry the old King's statue on horseback of brass was bought and to be set up at Charing Cross."

Of all the great impostors in the literary field none for sheer precociousness can compare with Thomas Chatterton, the poet. He was one of many of the "Grub Street writers" of the eighteenth century who indulged in confidence tricks.

Grub Street was the former name of a London street in the ward of Cripplegate, leading out of Fore Street, Moorfields. Dr. Samuel Johnson said it was "much inhabited by writers of small histories, dictionaries and temporary poems; whence any mean production is called *grubstreet*."

Perhaps the doctor spoke from bitter experience, for

his sneers cannot hide the fact that he was himself taken in by one of them. Richard Savage, an eighteenth century poet, claimed to be the natural son of the fourth Earl Rivers and the Countess of Macclesfield. On the strength of this story, which was never wholly disproved, he gained financial help from a wide circle of influential people, including, so it is said, Dr. Johnson himself. Ultimately, it was generally assumed that Savage was just a con-man, competent though he might be as a poet. As one last trick in 1728 he wrote a poem called *The Bastard*, in which he attacked his reputed mother. He was then induced to keep silent by being given a pension of two hundred pounds a year. All this seems to have been of little avail, for he died in a debtors' prison at Bristol.

But Thomas Chatterton was in an entirely different category. He, curiously enough, when considering the story of Richard Savage, was born in Bristol in 1752. When he was five years old he was considered to be so stupid and dull-witted that his teachers deemed him to be incapable of learning how to read or write. Perhaps there is in the make-up of the highly individualist confidence trickster a finely balanced composition of warring qualities—of dullness and laziness on the one hand and a spark of genius and latent cunning on the other. Chatterton had all these attributes in his character, and we are told that "it was not until his latent powers were roused by being shown the illuminated capitals of an old French manuscript, that he became anxious to acquire learning." Suddenly he blossomed and, as a boy of eight at Colston's Bluecoat School in Bristol, made his first attempts at verse. In his holidays he spent long hours alone in a tiny room at the top of his home studying old parchments which he had extracted from the muniments room at St. Mary Redcliffe, amusing himself by weaving fantasies around them. Probably through being bored with his first job—an apprenticeship to a Bristol attorney

—he started to plan his forgeries.

He publicised his long-term plan by talking knowingly about a mysterious fifteenth century monk named Rowley, the supposed friend and confessor of a Bristol merchant named Canynge. He even read to his friends poems which, he said, were composed by Rowley. Then in October, 1768, when the new Bristol Bridge was opened, he contributed to *Farley's Bristol Journal* an article which reproduced what purported to be "a description of the Friars first passing over the old bridge: taken from an ancient manuscript."

This was his first forgery. Subsequently he produced various poems of quite exceptional beauty, written in the style of fifteenth century England. He claimed that these poems were copied from parchments which his father had found in a large box in a room over the north side of Redcliffe Church. Soon Chatterton acquired quite a reputation in literary circles and he gave up his post in Bristol to seek literary fame in London. Here he submitted the Rowley poems to Horace Walpole, who seems initially to have been completely convinced that they were genuine. Chatterton followed up by sending further manuscripts to Walpole, asking for financial assistance and patronage. Walpole then submitted the documents to experts who pronounced them as forgeries.

But Chatterton, who had had some small success with some of the pretended poems of Rowley which had been published, did not give in easily. In reply to Walpole he insisted on the genuineness of the poems and asked for the return of the documents. Long afterwards, Walpole, who could be churlish on occasions, sent them back, but without any comments. A few encouraging remarks at that stage might well have enabled Chatterton to pursue an honourable career without forgery and even have saved his life. For there is no doubt that, whatever misuse he had made of his talents. Chatterton was a very promising poet and not just a literary forger.

To understand why the youth practised this deception one must realise that all poets and very many writers in the eighteenth century depended upon patronage for their very existence. Chatterton could only acquire patrons by drawing attention to himself. In 1770 he went to London, hoping to succeed as a poet, but after six months he had only earned five pounds. He concealed his abject poverty from his widowed mother and sister by sending them handsome presents while he himself was starving. After destroying all his papers he ended his life on August 24th, 1770, by swallowing a dose of arsenic in water.

Many of the Grub Street writers obtained money in advance from various noblemen for projects which they either never undertook or never finished. They took advantage of the subscription system which prevailed at that time, that is, the obtaining of subscriptions for a work in advance of publication. Charles Churchill, the poet, who was luckier in having very wealthy patrons, summed up the practice rather neatly in his poem, *The Ghost*:

"He for subscribers baits his hook,
And takes their cash—but where's the book?"

Shakespeare has inspired more confidence tricksters than anyone else in the literary world. This has undoubtedly been due partly to the fact that he is one of the most widely known writers of all time, but also to the lack of information about his life and the still raging controversy as to whether he really wrote his own plays, or if these were composed by Bacon, Marlowe or some other Elizabethan scribe. The truth is that the Shakespearian plays and sonnets are a rich field for the literary impostor.

Horace Walpole, the same man who had decried the forgery of Chatterton, was one of the first to suggest that Lord Verulam (Francis Bacon) was the author of the

Shakespeare plays, introducing the theory of Baconism in a series of essays entitled *Historic Doubts*. However, Walpole merely timorously engaged in sophistry, not full scale deception. It was not until 1848 that an English writer named Joseph G. Hart and an American, Delia Bacon, combined to found a cult of Baconism. They were followed by an erratic Minnesota politician, Ignatius T. T. Donnelly, who was convinced that if Lord Verulam had written the Shakespearean plays, he would have left within them some messages in cipher, bearing in mind that he was an enthusiastic cryptographer. After much juggling with texts and the counting of words, mixed with a certain amount of imaginative interpretation, Donnelly wrote a book called *The Great Cryptogram*, describing how Bacon had been the author of the plays, but had concealed this because of his political ambitions and that some of his works could have been deemed treasonable. It did not take long for scholars to tear the Donnelly theory to pieces.

A rather more daring and skilful exploitation of the Shakespearean cult was that of a boy, William Henry Ireland. It all started with the preface which Edmund Malone wrote to his edition of Shakespeare's plays, published in 1790. This embodied the results of many years of patient research and he suggested that as there was "proof that the executor of Shakespeare's will left a library and manuscripts behind him" so there could be descendants of Shakespeare among the present generation who, if they searched diligently, might be able "to rescue from the limbo of forgotten things valuable new manuscripts".

A new discovery of Shakespearian papers was announced for exhibition in Norfolk Street, London, in 1794. So convinced were some scholars who saw the papers of their authenticity that they undertook the publication of them by public subscription at four guineas a copy—a large sum for those days.

When the book was published Edmund Malone read it and immediately decided it was palpably a daring forgery. Slowly the story of this imposture came to light. William Henry Ireland, the perpetrator of the forgery, was a sixteen-year old apprentice to a London conveyancer when he plotted his charade. The son of a fervid antique book collector and devotee of Shakespeare, young William took advantage of the fact that he worked in an office which had access to vast quantities of old deeds. From one of these he cut a piece of parchment and wrote on it what purported to be a mortgage deed bearing Shakespeare's signature. This he showed to his father, who accepted it as being authentic.

Having chalked up a preliminary success with this trial run at forgery, young Ireland decided to be more ambitious. His aim was to write a Shakespearian play and to pass it off as a missing work of the Bard's. Astoundingly difficult though this self-imposed task might seem to an inexperienced youth, Ireland possessed certain qualifications for this audacious literary hoax. He had studied Shakespeare as a boy rather more thoroughly than most of his age, he had learned to interest himself in many aspects of the Bard's work through his father's enthusiasm, had visited all the places associated with Shakespeare both in Stratford-on-Avon and London. But, perhaps most important of all, he had sought out and talked to Chatterton's sister and questioned her in great detail about her brother's own methods of forgery. Doubtless Chatterton was the source of Ireland's inspiration, and by talking to the dead poet's sister he determined to profit from his knowledge of the reasons for Chatterton being detected.

Then Ireland set about collecting as secretively as possible the material for his plot. He acquired blank sheets of ancient paper and bribed a chemist to mix for him an ink which would pass for the kind that was used in Elizabethan times. In one sense Chatterton was a cleverer forger than Ireland: he had to concoct his forgeries without having the money to buy the right kind of materials. But he compensated for this by being a real poet.

Long afterwards, when Malone had unmasked his forgeries, Ireland made a lengthy confession of how he set about deceiving the greatest Shakespearian experts of the day. After his first effort of forging the deed, his second attempt was to compose and write in a style modelled on Shakespeare's own caligraphy "a Protestant Profession of Faith by William Shakespeare" in about three hundred words.

This "Profession of Faith" was again accepted by experts as a marvellous and genuine find and Ireland followed this up with extracts from what were said to be the original manuscript of *Hamlet* and—most outrageously impudent touch of all—a box containing what were solemnly sworn to be locks of Shakespeare's hair. Boswell, always a romantic, went into such raptures about the last two finds that he asked to be allowed to kiss the locks of hair, while the Prince of Wales also went to see this "Shakespearian collection".

Amazed and gratified by the extent of his success, Ireland now embarked on the most ambitious forgery of all—the writing of a play which could be attributed to the Bard.

"When the idea of writing a play first took possession of my mind," confessed Ireland, "I continued for some days undecided as to the subject most appropriate to the purpose; when a large drawing . . . representing Rowena in the act of presenting wine to Vortigern . . . suddenly attracted my attention. In consequence, when alone I took down Mr. Ireland's [his father] edition of *Holinshed's Chronicle*, and referred to the story of Vortigern as related by that historian; when, conceiving it apt to my purpose, I immediately planned the outline of the play."

The drama of *Vortigern and Rowena* in blank verse was

the outcome of this inspiration. Then came the final coup—the production of the play at Drury Lane Theatre by Sheridan himself. The dramatist himself must have had some initial doubts about the work, for he told Ireland : "There are certainly some bold ideas, but they are crude and undigested. It is very odd : one would be led to think that Shakespeare must have been very young when he wrote the play."

It was then agreed that Sheridan would pay three hundred pounds down for the play, Ireland's father being made the trustee for his son, who was, of course, still under age by the law of the times. The opening night was a sell-out, but the play was almost unanimously derided by the critics.

Young Ireland had, however, planned other plays to succeed *Vortigern and Rowena*. The story of Henry II and Fair Rosamund was one theme which appealed to him and he admitted later that he wished he had written this play first as "it was allowed by all to be a more finished composition than the *Vortigern*."

When eventually his deceptions were laid bare by Malone, the youth was honourable enough to take the whole blame upon himself, for what really troubled him was that his father had been attacked as the prime instigator of the forgeries. He exonerated his parent completely, adding wistfully: "Had the play *Vortigern* succeeded with the public, and the manuscripts been acknowledged as genuine, it was my intention to have completed a series of plays from the reign of William the Conqueror to that of Queen Elizabeth, that is to say, I should have planned a drama on every reign the subject of which had not been treated of by Shakespeare."

What he seems to have failed to realise is that by the time he had reached Richard I, if not long before, somebody would have wanted to know why all these manuscripts did not turn up at once instead of at regular intervals.

The man who made literary forgery profitable was undoubtedly J. T. Wise, born in the middle of the nineteenth century, who started his career as an office-boy and later became a partner in the same firm. Wise, like Ireland's father, was a keen book collector and he made a reputation for himself as an expert on antique books and as a finder of rare first editions. His Ashley Library collection of first editions was bought for £60,000 by the British Museum after his death.

Such was Wise's fame as a bibliophil that he was sought after by such men as Edmund Gosse, Browning and Swinburne. His first step towards fraud came when he started to publish facsimile reprints of first editions of Shelley's works. This was, of course, perfectly legal as the facsimiles were clearly marked as such, but they were so splendidly executed that Wise then had the idea of forging first editions. After that his method of forgery was simplicity itself: he reproduced facsimiles of first editions, but left out his own name and imprint and any mention of their being facsimiles. Ultimately it was only a question of treating the books to give a semblance of age. Wise undoubtedly knew all about the forgeries of Chatterton and Ireland, and avoided making their mistake of trying to forge something that was really old. He concentrated on turning out bogus first editions of early nineteenth century works.

It is almost impossible to say how many forgeries of this type Wise actually perpetrated, or how many may still be lying around in unsuspected places. Even a Wise forgery is worth a fair sum as a literary curiosity today. One of his earliest efforts was to "discover" a small volume of poems by Elizabeth Barratt Browning, entitled *Sonnets by E.B.B. Not For Publication, 1847*, ostensibly published by her friend, Mary Mitford. The last-named had died, so she could neither deny nor confirm this and Wise's story was that he had obtained some copies of this book (of which only a few were printed for private circulation only) from a Dr. Bennett, who had died just afterwards. He backed up this tale by a carefully detailed piece of "evidence" based on his own close study of the lives and works of Elizabeth Browning and her husband. To a few close friends in the literary world Wise offered copies of the book at ten pounds a time, but, having well publicised this fantastic imposture, he then sold another copy in New York for £250, a high sum for a modern first edition in those days.

For many years this game of forgery went on and, having bamboozled the experts with bogus copies of first editions of the dead—Wordsworth, Tennyson and Dickens among them—Wise went on to forge those of the living, including Kipling, William Morris, Ruskin, Stevenson and Swinburne. What helped Wise was his knowledge of the psychology of the average collector of first editions. So eager were many to boast the possession of rare editions that they would gladly accept the assurance of almost anyone that they were being offered the genuine article. Then again, Wise understood perfectly the best way of exploiting the homosexual underground of the literary world of those days. Whether this was mixed with a mild form of blackmail one does not know, but Edmund Gosse was certainly one of a number of his homosexual cronies and fellow-conspirators.

It was Gosse who had helped to build up the evidence for Wise in the first instance in connection with the Elizabeth Browning book. But in the end both men were caught out years after their deaths by two young members of the London antiquarian book trade, John Carter and Graham Pollard in a book entitled *An Enquiry into the Nature of Certain Nineteenth Century Pamphlets*, published in 1934. Yet Wise, like young Ireland, was not entirely doing all this solely to make money. Probably what gave him a tremendous feeling of exhilaration was the sense of being regarded as a prince of bibliophils among his contemporaries. No doubt the money he obtained from the sale of his forgeries was used to buy genuine first editions and rare books, for there were many such among his collection when he died.

8

MESSIAHS AND THEIR LOVE FEASTS

AN UNUSUAL form of confidence trickery manifested itself in many parts of the world in the late eighteenth and early nineteenth centuries. It was an evangelistic philosophy that was both religious and erotic, and soon movements of this nature began to spring up simultaneously in Germany, Russia, France, England and North America. Yet, as far as one can tell, there was no direct association between any of them. The leaders and self-appointed prophets of these various groups regarded themselves as Messiahs.

First of these was a German gamekeeper named Hans Rosenfeld. The line he took in spreading his own particular gospel in Prussia and the neighbouring states was that Christianity was a deception and that its priests were impostors. By debunking the old religion, he sought to put a new one—his own—in its place and he might have been successful if he had not attempted to bring politics into it as well. For, having denounced the Christian religion, he proceeded to attack the despotic government of Frederick the Great and stated publicly that it was his intention to depose that ruler.

"When I have deposed the Emperor," he said, "I shall set up a Council of twenty-four Elders and with them I shall rule the whole world. At the chosen moment when the Emperor sets out to provoke me, I shall use my powers to down him."

The Prussian authorities showed an almost benevolent indifference to the seditious teachings of this gamekeeper turned prophet. For twenty years Rosenfeld was allowed to carry on his campaign with very little interference except for an occasional very brief spell of imprisonment for some breach of the peace. Frederick the Great could afford to be lenient.

Rosenfeld had stated that when he established his Council of Elders and assumed power in Prussia seven Messianic Seals were to be opened and their contents made known to the world. Seven "angels" were to open the seals and in this context Rosenfeld sought to combine his new "religion" with personal gratification and well-being. He asked his followers to provide him with seven beautiful girls who were to fill the office of "Angels of the Seal". Until the time arrived for the Seals to be opened these seven girls were to become his mistresses and support him by their own work.

It was a splendid life while it lasted and this blatant confidence trick might well have continued until Rosenfeld's death, but for the fact that he rashly asked one of his most devoted followers to give up three of his daughters as "Angels." This man grew impatient with Rosenfeld's promise of the great life that was to come and which, with the passing of each year, seemed no nearer. But while he was impatient about the progress towards Utopia, he remained a firm believer in Rosenfeld's Messianic role. He decided to go to the Emperor and to provoke him to act against Rosenfeld. Then, he felt sure, their beloved Messiah would conjure up his supernatural powers and depose Frederick.

The Emperor reacted promptly at last. This time he ordered Rosenfeld to be arrested and put on trial for treasonous activities against the state. The gamekeeper gave no sign of his self-claimed supernatural powers to his now dismayed followers. In 1782 he was tried and sentenced to be whipped and imprisoned for life at Spandau. Though he twice appealed against this sentence, it was finally carried out.

A different kind of imposture was that performed by Joanna Southcott, a prophetic visionary who was born in the Devonshire village of Dittisham in 1750, the daughter of a small farmer. She was said to have been a child of almost angelic behaviour, always willing to help others, delighting in studying the Scriptures in her spare time and was "accustomed to apply directly to Heaven for advice".

Perhaps only a psychiatrist could tell us whether Joanna deceived herself more than she did other people. Certainly, she was capable of deceiving others and convincing herself of her supernatural powers. She believed that she was the leader of a genuine new prophetic movement, but in propagating this idea she entered on a career of imposture that raised more than 14,000 adherents in one mission alone.

Yet as a child she also revealed traits which to some extent should have warned others of that hint of imposture and vanity which lay beneath the outward mask of piety. She had a fondness for wearing fine clothes and she liked to show herself off in them. She also had love affairs as a young girl, while at the same time professing horror at other people's promiscuity.

Then in 1792, when she was forty-two, Joanna claimed to have heard voices—"words so dreadful that they made me tremble," she said. She began to write down what the "voices" told her and started to make prophecies. Many of these concerned political or world events and in several cases subsequent events confirmed them. On one occasion she predicted that the Bishop of Exeter, who was then in excellent health, would not live until Christmas. He died on December 12th. When Lord

Malmesbury announced his intention of going to Paris to sue for peace, Joanna forecast that he would be unsuccessful. This, too, was borne out by events. Nor was this merely intelligent forecasting, for the odds were that he would succeed.

Her predictions as much as her desire to lead a religious crusade won followers for Joanna Southcott. William Sharp, one of her closest followers, stated that "from the end of 1792 to the end of 1794 her writings were sealed up with great caution and remained secure till they were conveyed by me to High House, Paddington, and the box which contained them was opened in the beginning of January, 1803. Her writings were examined during seven days and the result of this long scrutiny was that unanimous decision of twenty-three persons appointed by divine command, as well as of thirty-five others that were present, that her calling was of God."

Joanna insisted that she was the "woman" named in *Revelations*, Chapter VII, charged with "sealing the Elect". The object of her mission was to bring forth a son, the Shiloh, promised to be born of a virgin, and this event was looked forward to by her followers with extraordinary enthusiasm and credulity. The purpose of her prophecies and life was to announce to the world that the second coming of Christ was drawing near.

She was also one of the first Women's Liberators and it was in her propagation of this cause that she carried her imposture to excess. For, quite clearly, though in a different and much more subtle way, Joanna was a masquerading Messiah like Rosenfeld. She insisted that God always chose a woman when he wanted things done. And had not Christ himself chosen a girl from a village when he first came to speak to the people? Now her "voices" told her that she was "the true and faithful Bride".

Joanna's campaign for recruits was a kind of spiritual

protection racket. The "protection" was offered for all who subscribed their names to the cause and paid over money. It took the form of a folded paper, endorsed with the person's name and secured with the impression of Joanna's seal in red wax, a talisman consisting of a circle enclosing the initials "J.C.", with a star above and below and the following inscription: "The Sealed of the Lord, the Elect, Precious, Man's Redemption, to inherit the tree of life, to be made heirs of God and joint-heirs of Jesus Christ." This was authenticated by the signature of the prophetess in her curiously illegible characters.

In 1801 Joanna Southcott published her first book, a ninepenny pamphlet entitled *The Strange Effects of Faith*. It had an amazing success and won for Joanna many followers of distinction, including Thomas Foley, a Fellow of Jesus College, Cambridge, Halhed, an oriental scholar who was Member of Parliament for Lymington, a number of clergymen and even some hard-headed business magnates. Soon she was invited to London to win adherents in the capital. From there she travelled far and wide winning recruits until in October, 1808, the newspapers carried headlines reading:

"Shocking Disclosure of the Morals of Joanna Southcott's Followers."

For a long time there had been suspicions about the motives of some of those who had been collecting money for Joanna's crusade. One of these was Mary Bateman, ostensibly a sedate and soberly dressed Quaker, but actually a thief and abortionist. When she heard of Joanna Southcott she saw the possibilities of exploiting this growing community, bought a seal and posed as a member of the sect. But eventually Bateman was arrested for the murder of one, Rebecca Perigo, and sentenced to death. On the gallows Mary Bateman declared that at the very last moment an angel would descend from heaven and rescue her. After she had been hanged, more than 2,000 people paid threepence each to look at her body.

Joanna strongly resented charges that she was making money for herself by selling the seals. Nothing was ever proved against her in this respect, though a number of her followers were detected in various acts of fraud and obtaining money under false pretences. In the end, she stopped the sale of seals and demanded that all those that were still unsold should be called in.

Suddenly, when she was sixty-four years old, Joanna's "voices" told her to prepare for the mystic birth. "Order twelve gowns for thy wedding," was one command from on high. Then came another prophecy from the same mysterious quarter: "This year thou shalt bear a son by the power of the Most High."

While others suspected this might be the onset of madness, Joanna calmly said that this merely confirmed what she had always known that she was the woman in the twelfth chapter of *Revelations* referred to in the verse: "And there appeared a great wonder in heaven, a woman clothed with the sun, and the moon under her feet, and upon her head a crown of twelve stars . . . And she brought forth a man child who was to rule all the nations with a rod of iron and her child was caught up unto God and to his throne."

In other words, Shiloh was her unborn baby!

A few months later Joanna announced that she had been medically examined and pronounced pregnant. Boldly, she asked the Prince Regent, the Dukes of Gloucester and Kent and the Archbishop of Canterbury to send their own doctors "to pass judgement whether they think it is likely for such an event to take place."

Naturally, she insisted that this was a virgin birth, a miraculous birth, in fact. A number of doctors came to examine her and Dr. Richard Reece, author of the *Medical Guide*, gave it as his opinion that "she is with child" and he added that he had brought "nine medical practitioners" to see her and that six of them had pronounced her pregnant.

Controversy raged in the newspapers. The doctors who believed that she was pregnant marvelled only at such a thing happening at the age of sixty-four—they felt sure that somewhere there must be a human father. But Joanna's followers accepted totally that this must be a miraculous, virgin birth and that Joanna was incapable of being unchaste. Preparations for the baby Shiloh went ahead, a satinwood crib costing £200 being specially made, while leather-bound Bibles, christening mugs and bibs were turned out by the score. The incredulous suggested that a pregnant woman from a nearby workhouse had been hidden in the house in which Joanna was lodging and that her baby would be brought forward as Joanna's when it was born. Then the house in which she lived was attacked by a mob and Joanna had to move elsewhere. She spent most of her time in bed, "eating much, but praying little", it was observed by some. Then she surprisingly decreed that Shiloh must have a foster-father when he was born and that she required a husband speedily. Several applied following her appeal and finally she chose one, John Smith, a steward of the Earl of Darnley, to whom she was married in her bedroom.

After this there was anti-climax, then tragedy. Soon every trace of pregnancy vanished, even according to the doctors who had previously said otherwise. Joanna appeared deeply shocked and fell into a coma. A few days later she died. Yet the hard core of her followers believed she would come back to life. They felt sure their Prophetess would survive. What did, of course, survive was the Southcottian Movement. Joanna's community continued to grow and an offspring, the Panacea Society, was formed. Joanna had left behind a locked wooden box which was not to be opened until a time of national crisis and then only in the presence of all the bishops of

England. Demands for the box to be opened during the Crimean War and World War I were resisted by the bishops, but it was opened in 1927 in the presence of one bishop who found it contained unimportant papers, a lottery ticket, a night-cap and a novelette entitled *An Adventure in Greenwich Park*. But another box opened later was found to contain genuine papers written by Joanna.

The Prophetess from Devonshire proved unique in one respect: she continues to be a source of inspiration long after her death. For the Panacea Society is recognised as a *bona fide* charity by the Charity Commissioners along with many other bizarre societies such as the British Goat Society and the Maid's Money of Guildford.

The later "Messiahs" who imposed on large numbers of people on both sides of the Atlantic in the nineteenth century were more worldly and business-minded. They also paid much more attention to fostering the erotic undertones of their respective "religions."

In Germany, Archdeacon Ebel, founder of the Pietists, vulgarly called the Muckers, pronounced 1836 as the opening year of the personal reign of Christ. Ebel created what was in effect a Female Church, and his chief disciple was a Prussian countess of Königsberg, Ida von der Gröben. A widow of considerable beauty and charm, she entered into a pact with two other distinguished women to watch over the Archdeacon at all times and to guard him from temptation. In this church women not only heard the confessions of male sinners, but had the power to grant them absolution, or to inflict penance.

This was "Women's Lib" in religion with a vengeance and it has not been matched even in modern times. By giving full scope to the female sex, Ebel showed that remarkable psychological insight which is the hall-mark of the true impostor. His three female disciples condemned drinking, smoking and the taking of snuff by men. "To teach and to scold was the woman's part in the Female Church," wrote William Hepworth Dixon. "They were supposed to understand the masculine nature perfectly and every man in these circles who wanted guidance, comfort and instruction had to wait upon them. The ladies are said to have been very hard and searching as to secret sins and to have wrung confessions from the most unwilling penitents . . . they sometimes went beyond the bounds of fact, using their nimble fancies to suggest offences, such as might have been committed in thought, if not in act. The men, it is said, found out that the more they confessed the more they would be petted and praised."

And, of course, this led to other things. There was kissing and hugging always going on between male and female in Ebel's church services, but it was all rather a child-like game played out between the sexes. Eventually the Ebelian sect as laid down by its male founder decreed that since God could do no wrong, nor could his (her?) children. But it was really a snob Church that aspired to be the most fashionable in Prussia. What did Ebel achieve by his conmanship? Well, when ultimately all three of his disciples formed one united household with him, Ebel was able to describe Countess Ida as his "first wife, representing the spirit of Light," Emilie von Scrotter as his "second wife, representing the spirit of Darkness" and the third as his legal wife, representing "the spirit of Union". It would seem that the legal wife's main functions were to work in the kitchen and the still-room and not to share in the delights, spiritual or otherwise, of Ebel's relations with the other two.

Thus Ebel had achieved one of the biggest cons of all time. Posing as a supporter and indeed initiator of "Women's Lib" in religion, he had conned the females into serving him in every possible manner.

About the same time a number of religious sects with

erotic aspects sprang up in America. The theme was much the same in essence as the theory of "spiritual wives" propounded by Ebel. Conmen appeared in various pioneer communities in America. The Reverend Jarvis Rider, a preacher who had the reputation of having had a succession of spirit-brides, deemed it to be "a necessary consequence of the Second Coming". Hiram Sheldon, who preached salvation from sin, thought it was "the last refuge of virtue in a profligate world", an idea he put into practice by seeking in Sophia Cook, one of his prettier disciples, a kinship of soul which he had failed to find with his own lawful wife. Sydney Rigdon, the pastor of a church at Kirtland, Ohio, a hot revivalist, had startled his congregation with his insistence that holy men had a right "to woo and win for themselves brides of the spirit as well as of the flesh".

But it was on the shores of Lake Oneida, in the farmlands of Oneida County, and especially in the district surrounding the Cayuga and Oneida Lakes, that the greatest furore was created. Here in a beerhouse the new gospel of spiritual wives had been proclaimed and the young factory girls had been flattered and thrilled into acceptance of the utopian delights promised them. "When a man becomes conscious that his soul is saved," declared John Humphrey Noyes, the founder of what he called Pauline Communism, "the first thing he sets about is to find his Paradise and his Eve".

Noyes had been a Congregational minister before he set about forming his own cult, culminating in the organisation of a community of Bible Communists at Oneida Creek. However, it was in England rather than America that the next religious confidence trickster appeared in the person of Henry James Prince, a doctor of medicine and a clergyman of the Church of England. His early reputation was that of a prude and killjoy, obsessed with sin and a predilection for saving the souls of his female parishioners. By the end of a year's curacy at Charlinch in Somerset he could boast that "I have saved four souls, a widow of eighty, a wicked old crone of seventy-four, a farmer's wife and a milkmaid having come to me for conversion and ghostly counsel".

In fact, Prince's partiality for the females in his parish caused dissension and suspicion. It was not long before services were broken up by riots and women, prevented from going to evening prayer meetings by their menfolk, threatened to leave home. Prince was asked to resign his curacy. He went to another parish in Suffolk and again public opinion forced him to quit. He then broke away from the orthodox Church and formed what he called the Abode of Love at Spaxton in Somerset.

Here Prince's latent rascality peeped through his piety and his motives became somewhat clearer to a discerning observer. The Abode of Love was to be a place of safety and security from the outside world where he could found his own cult, to be financed by wealthy women, indulge in the luxury of "spiritual wives" and be the absolute ruler of a small but carefully chosen community. His first wife, Martha, had left him some money and he persuaded his second wife, Julia, to part with her annuity of eighty pounds a year. But he still needed much more money to run his lavish establishment.

One of his first methods of raising funds and supporters was by proclaiming the imminence of the end of the world. He told a congregation of a hundred at Weymouth that the time had come for "winnowing the world, for separating the wheat from the chaff". The day of judgement had come. The lost were lost for ever, but the saved would be with him.

And the money slowly trickled into his pockets. What Prince offered for the few—the wealthy few, let it be noted—was an earthly paradise under his control. Some wealthy ladies sold their shares and their land to join him. His principal capture was the five unmarried daughters of a retired merchant who had left them £6,000 each. He even persuaded three of them to throw in their lot with him entirely, to join the Abode of Love where they would be "saved".

How he managed to achieve this makes an admirable illustration of religious conmanship in action. He first sent for Harriet Nottidge and told her: "I have news for you. It will be to the glory of God if you will marry my young friend the Reverend Lewis Price."

Blushingly, but meekly, Harriet agreed to this proposal and to be sworn to secrecy meanwhile. For this was but the first part of Prince's carefully laid plan to secure for the sect all the sisters' money. With Agnes Nottidge, for whom he sent next, he changed his tactics.

"Agnes," he said, "God is about to confer on you a special blessing, but before I tell you what it is you must give me your word to obey the Lord and accept His gift."

For a moment even Agnes hesitated. Then, thinking that the acceptance of a blessing could do no harm, she gave her solemn promise. Then Prince dropped his bombshell: "In a few days you will marry 'Brother' Thomas [another clergyman friend]."

Agnes was at first shocked into silence, then she pleaded for time to think things over. But Prince was adamant: "In this matter," he replied, "you must think not of the world, or of yourself, but of God."

"But," said Agnes, who was less malleable than her sister, "there is my mother to consult and lawyers, too."

"God is your father and mother," rebuked the implacable Prince. "And why should you need lawyers to deal with God's business?"

"Well, there is the question of children," blushingly replied Agnes.

"You will have no children," answered Prince. "Your marriage with our brother will be spiritual only."

Agnes saw no end to this argument, but, unlike her

sister Harriet, she went away with misgivings. A few days later Clara, the third sister, was persuaded to marry William Cobbe, another of Prince's allies, and so three females joined Prince's band and contributed towards the building and maintenance of the Abode of Love. Agnes held out longest, but she succumbed in the end.

Thus was born the sect of the Agapemonites, so named after the *Agapetae*, a group of third-century ascetic women who, under vows of virginity, contracted spiritual marriage with monks and attended to their wants. The practice became widespread and led to scandals arising out of the love feasts in which they indulged.

Prince became an absolute dictator of the Abode of Love. When Agnes Thomas persuaded her husband to take her away for a holiday, Prince sent him a letter, saying: "Brother Thomas, I command you to arise and return."

The Abode of Love comprised a spacious mansion of some twenty bedrooms when Prince originally took it over. Within a few years it had developed into almost a self-contained hamlet in its own grounds, for in addition to the large house, a row of picturesque cottages was acquired, as well as a farm, granary and stables. It was run on efficient business lines from the day of its inception in 1847. The farm supplied most of their needs and the "Brothers" and "Sisters" lived affluently, as the revenue from the trust which Prince had set up enabled him to keep a large and well-stocked cellar of choice wines.

William Hepworth Dixon, who visited the Abode during this period, recalled that "A woman brought in a tray with biscuits and two decanters, one full of a good dry sherry, the other of a sweet, new port, which she laid down on the table, bidding me help myself and went out."

There was a "church" as well, created out of the largest room of the mansion. It had stained-glass windows and such incongruous touches as "a large red sofa set near a blazing fire . . . a billiard table and the sacred symbol of the Lamb and Dove, flanked by a rack of billiard-cues." The Agapemonites apparently used the church as a recreation hall as well.

One day Prince announced that he had "died in myself and become filled with the Holy Spirit;" But, he declared, if he was to purge the whole community from sin, a virgin must be found, a bride of the Lamb, someone who was young, beautiful and pure. He claimed that he had no idea who the bride of the Lamb would be, but that God would reveal her to him in His own good time. Among the inmates of the Abode of Love had been a widow and her young daughter. The mother had died, leaving her orphan girl in Prince's charge, little knowing that the lascivious priest had already coveted her. But as the days and weeks passed nobody seemed to suspect Prince's real intentions: all accepted that the identity of the "Bride" would be dramatically revealed by God in his own good time.

At last the "Beloved One", as Prince was known in the community, announced that the day had come and all were summoned to the church. He had a great sense of theatre and, as he entered the church, soft music from the organ filled the room and the cloying scent of incense issued from a score of tapers. Prince left nothing to chance; every device which he could charge with atmosphere and emotion, mysticism and a sensuous grandiloquence had been thought of, even to the extent of dimming the lights to a shade of amber which fell in a circle of radiance just above the altar.

When he was opposite Zoe Paterson, the orphan girl, he took her hand in his and gave her what he described as the Seraphic Kiss and in a low voice declared that his union with her was a mark of "God's love for the flesh".

There was no ceremony. The onlookers meekly accepted what had taken place, including Prince's ageing wife. There was a peal on the organ, the church was ablaze with lights. Zoe Paterson, who was only just sixteen, was too frightened and shy to speak. Prince led her away at once to his private apartments. It was quickly obvious that this mystic union was certainly not being conducted purely on a spiritual basis. "Sister" Zoe gave birth to a child.

This incident created a split in the ranks of the Agapemonites. The Reverend Lewis Price and his wife left the community and Prince was now an unfrocked clergyman who was loathed in the village of Spaxton. The community of what had been 120 dwindled to less than sixty. Prince ordered several of those left to undertake the work of domestic servants and gardeners as a penance.

Prince himself died in 1899 and he was buried in the gardens of the Abode of Love. It was not long before he was succeeded by another fast-talking confidence trickster who proclaimed himself a Messiah. This was John Hugh Smyth-Pigott, who as a young man had left the Merchant Navy to join the Church of England. All the time, however, he secretly dreamed of founding a free-love Utopia in which he should be the ruler. And if the Early Christians could accept such pagan rites as the love feasts, he thought that there could be a precedent for his own ideas if he set about this cautiously.

It was for this reason that he decided to become a clergyman. On a visit to Dublin he met the secretary of the Agapemonites (Douglas Hamilton), who told him he had come in quest of a new Messiah to lead the community at Spaxton. Smyth-Pigott, according to Hamilton's own account of their meeting, seemed to take the matter out of the secretary's hands. "Tell them the Heavenly Bridegroom has been found," the young curate told Hamilton. "Henceforth the Agapemone has a new leader. Let that be your message."

And, as if to stifle any possible hesitation on Hamilton's

part, he added imperiously: "That is my first command. From now on I expect obedience from all my followers."

Then, perhaps anxious to be tactful as well as masterful, he said: "You are my first messenger and you must always remain at my side as the most trusted of my followers".

Smyth-Pigott decided that the Abode of Love needed a metropolitan church as the show-piece of the sect. He chose the Ark of the Covenant Church in Clapton and from here he proclaimed himself Messiah in 1902. Until this time the church had only attracted the interest of a small group of Nonconformists, but from September 7th, 1902, it suddenly became the most notorious in the land. Intoxicated by his success in acquiring the leadership of the Spaxton community, Smyth-Pigott announced: "I am the Messiah. In me you behold Christ in the flesh and through me you shall know your salvation".

On the following Sunday more than 6,000 people arrived outside the church to await the arrival of the man who had called himself the Messiah. When Smyth-Pigott arrived, he was greeted by boos and hisses and after the service he had to be escorted away to safety by the police. Donations to the church gradually found their way into the coffers of the Agapemonites at Spaxton. The new leader soon indicated that the community needed to be more self-supporting. "The farm and gardens have been allowed to fall into decay," he stated. "There are at the Abode far too many old people, not enough has been done to bring in younger members in recent years. We must double our membership within the next few years and I intend, when possible, to bring in recruits from overseas."

While Smyth-Pigott himself lived lavishly in the mansion, ministered to by the "Sisters", he banished his wife Catherine to a small cottage on the estate and made it clear that she must set an example to all by performing the most humble of domestic duties. She was forbidden ever to come to her husband's private apartments.

The new Messiah divided the inmates of the Abode into three classes. The lowest class were called "helpmates of God"; they were really servants and had to perform such tasks as cleaning, cooking and washing, having passed an initiation ceremony in which they had to swear allegiance to the "Beloved One". After a period of probation they could, if the "Beloved One" approved, be promoted to the second class in which they were relieved of their menial duties and were in turn waited upon themselves. When they had passed through a further period of probation, they might hope to aspire to the highest class, notably that of the youngest and best-looking members of the community. In this way the "Beloved One" ensured that he was surrounded by a group of women from whom he could in due course choose his "soul-brides". It is significant that whereas Prince had allotted some of the highest positions in the Agapemonite hierarchy to men, Smyth-Pigott sought to eliminate men from the highest class and to relegate them to lesser posts in the establishment.

When a female member was finally admitted to the highest class of all, the vague generalisations about spiritual love were discarded and she was enjoined by the "Beloved One" to love her sisters and, above all, to love him. It was pointed out that spiritual love was another form of probation for the highest privilege of all, that of becoming a "Bride of the Lamb". Subtly, she was told that in certain circumstances sexual intercourse with the "Beloved One" was the most sacred act of all. By swearing each "Sister" to absolute secrecy on these matters Smyth-Pigott managed for a very long time to maintain the myth that all his associations with the highest class were on a completely platonic plane. Once a week, after dinner, he summoned the "Sisters" of the highest class to the church and chose from them seven women who were to be his "spiritual brides" for each day of the following week. Wearing a white robe, embroidered with a design of the Lion of the fold of Judah, he called out the names of the women selected, said a brief prayer and then retired to his apartments, followed by the seven.

It says much for his eloquent powers of persuasion that he was able to lure into the Abode so many beautiful, young, well-educated and often wealthy women. The people of Spaxton who saw these women when they went out for rides by carriage, or to picnic and bathing parties at the seaside, described them as "gentry". The circle of soul-brides" increased from thirty to fifty-five and many of these contributed the whole of their possessions and money to the society.

Smyth-Pigott was more shrewd and practical than Prince. He set out to improve the image of the Abode in the minds of the villagers. Realising that the increase in the population of the Abode meant more business and prosperity for local shops, he urged members to spend their money in Spaxton rather than elsewhere, though insisting that the affairs of the society must never be discussed in the village. At the same time he used Hamilton, the society secretary, to spy on persons in the locality suspected of being hostile to the sect or too curious about its rites.

Smyth-Pigott claimed that the Agapemonite doctrine was essentially based on the earliest form of Christian teaching. The main factor in it was the Second Advent, belief in this being the cornerstone of Agapemonite thought and with it was linked acceptance of Smyth-Pigott as the Messiah. The "Beloved One" taught his flock that Adam came into contact with the Devil concealed within a woman's body and that, by the act of the Great Manifestation, and by taking "the Bride of the Lamb", he not only saved all believers in him, but drove out for all time the Evil Thing that had until then defiled the bodies of all human beings. Thus he paved the way for the coming of the Super Bride. At one time he actually employed a doctor (also a member) at the Abode to carry out regular examinations of the women in order to confirm and certify their claims to virginity.

But in July, 1904, Smyth-Pigott caused some chagrin and much surprise by choosing his "Bride of the Lamb" from outside the Abode and indeed from outside the membership of the society. Suddenly, and without any explanation as to how or where he found her, the "Beloved One" returned from one of his mysterious "pilgrimages to the wicked outside world" (as he phrased it), bringing with him a girl of twenty-one whom he solemnly announced was to be his "Chief Soul-Bride".

The newcomer was a Miss Ruth Anne Preece, a fascinatingly beautiful girl with pathetic large, brown eyes and an expression of exquisite innocence. Smyth-Pigott's wife seems to have accepted this announcement quite calmly. There was a midnight ritual to welcome Ruth, conducted by the Beloved One himself in the church, which was lit by eight silver lamps. The girl was then enthroned as Smyth-Pigott's consort. A year later, on June 23rd, 1905, Ruth gave birth to a son, who was christened Glory in the Abode, but was later more generally known by the name of David. His birth was duly registered and the name of the father given as "John Hugh Smyth-Pigott, priest in holy orders". The following year another child was born, this time being called Power. The birth of Ruth's two children gave rise to indignant gossip outside the Abode and eventually the Bishop of Bath and Wells ordered that Smyth-Pigott should be arraigned before a Consistory Court on charges of immorality. Smyth-Pigott refused to receive the summons or to appear before the Consistory Court. The case was heard in his absence and he was duly unfrocked and degraded from holy orders. Despite this, and in the face of hostile press criticism of the Abode of Love, the Agapemonites still carried on as usual. As for the "Beloved One", he tired of Ruth after she had borne him a third child and chose as her successor a young Russian girl who had been educated in England and just joined the community. But this girl managed to escape from the Abode after Smyth-Pigott had made advances to her. Sometime after this he decided that "Sister Ruth", who had become somewhat critical of his pursuit of other "Sisters", must be publicly degraded and another proclaimed his new principal "Soul-Bride" in her place.

So "Sister Ruth" was stripped of her robes by some of the other "Sisters" and left in front of the altar in a semi-nude condition at a ceremony stage-managed by Smyth-Pigott. "Sister Grace", another newcomer, was then appointed as his "Bride in Heaven". Ruth, however, declined to remain in the Abode after she was treated with harsh indifference by the other members. But as a last gesture of spite against her when she left, Smyth-Pigott prevented her from taking her children.

There were various other "Soul-Brides" during his long sojourn at Spaxton, the last one being "Sister Dora", who outlived him. In the later years Smyth-Pigott founded other Abodes of Love whenever opportunity presented itself, notably in France and Norway. He was a frequent visitor to the Norwegian Abode near Christiana and for some years a number of Norwegian girls used to pay annual visits to Spaxton. He died in 1927 and, like Prince before him, was buried in the grounds of the Abode of Love. The community was never the same without his leadership. Seances were actually held at the Abode with a view to obtaining "guidance" from his departed spirit, but all to no avail. The last comment on them in the words of a contemporary newspaper report was:

"The village people have been told that one evening, when his [Smyth-Pigott's] "Soul-Brides" were gathered in front of the gilded throne [on which he used to sit], the ghost of the dead "Messiah" suddenly appeared in a blaze of light. Among the faithful colonists who witnessed the apparition were young women who had dabbled in the occult. However, the shadow did not speak, but pointed to the empty throne and then faded out."

9

THE FORMOSAN STUDENT AND THE BARONET FROM NOWHERE

THE TWO most publicised impostors of the eighteenth and nineteenth centuries both chose to stage their imaginary points of entry to a gullible world from far distant places—George Psalmanazar from Formosa (or Taiwan, as it is better known today) and Arthur Orton from a wreck in the South Atlantic.

George Psalmanazar, who arrived in London in 1703, made perhaps the shrewdest choice, as Formosa was then an almost unknown island to the Western World. It was not surprising, therefore, that when he brought to London a letter of introduction from an army chaplain he was accepted at once as a genuine Formosan by people eager to hear more about this mysterious island off the coast of China. The Bishop of London received him with enthusiasm, especially as Psalmanazar presented him with an English Catechism translated into Formosan. Within a few weeks he was dining with Sir Hans Sloane, the famous physician, and the Prussian Ambassador, and being launched on London society.

George's story was that he was a native of Formosa and had been converted to Christianity. He had left the island at the age of nineteen. He could speak several languages and could also read and write Latin. Not unnaturally he was regarded as somewhat of a youthful prodigy from a heathen country. Archbishop Tennison, enormously impressed by the young man's Latin, persuaded him to write a book about Formosa.

His *Description of Formosa* was originally composed in Latin. It was published in English in 1704 and contained a grammar of the Formosan language which was a complete fabrication from beginning to end. The full title of the work was *An Historical and Geographical Description of Formosa, an Island subject to the Emperor of Japan*, dedicated to the Bishop of London. It told how the Japanese had invaded Formosa and occupied the country, despite the fact that the island was then a dependency of China and was not in fact formally ceded to Japan until 1895. Nevertheless, though a certain Father Fontenay criticised the book for making this mistake, Psalmanazar boldly replied that he had first-hand knowledge of what had happened whereas the Jesuit father did not. And he seems to have hoodwinked most people, for the book had such a large sale that a second edition was published the following year.

In his faked history of Formosa Psalmanazar took the view that the more sensational it was the bigger the sales would be. He described how the Formosans were instructed to build a temple and on its altar burn the hearts of 20,000 boys under the age of nine. This was good hot stuff to give the credulous, but even Psalmanazar knew that he had to explain somehow why the country did not become uninhabited through these sacrificial rites. So he made the Formosans a polygamous race and said that their first-born sons were all exempted from sacrifice.

Even in scholarly circles in London Psalmanazar's imposture remained undetected for a long time. It was only by careful probing by the critics that Psalmanazar's case could slowly be eroded. He himself made a stubborn and skilled fight against the doubters and sustained his hoax for seven years. Yet he made only twenty-two pounds from the sales of both editions of his book, a poor return for what must have been a lengthy, time-consuming piece of bogus scholarship. Where he benefited most was from the friendships with the famous and wealthy which his literary caper brought him. If he only made twenty-two pounds out of his work, he must have consumed ten times that number of hot dinners.

The truth about Psalmanazar was that he was born in the South of France sometime around 1679. His real name was never discovered. Most probably he came from the Midi, as a French clergyman who knew him in London said he spoke with "the accents of Gascony". Long afterwards he admitted that he came from poor parents, that he studied with Franciscans and Jesuits, from whom he learned Latin and some Greek and Hebrew. It seems reasonable to believe that he had more than a smattering of the last two languages as his bogus Formosan language seemed partly to have been based on Greek and Hebrew roots.

Early in life he became a nomad who lived on his wits, travelling from France across Europe into Germany and the Low Countries, curiously posing as an Irish student. Later he masqueraded as a Japanese student, possibly to avoid being conscripted into one of the continental armies, as he was rejected owing to his being classed as "a heathen". Yet, strangely, the next time he turned up in Holland, he joined a regiment of Germans under the name of Psalmanazar. He was still posing as a Japanese and, despite his European birth, convincing people he was an oriental. It must have been about this time that he first had the idea of posing as a Formosan, but what is less clear is why he did it. As far as can be deducted he had adopted his earlier poses solely to draw attention to himself, to feel he was noticed. Perhaps also he loved hoaxing as others like practical joking. But the adoption of the Formosan pose was something quite different. He seems to have realised that nobody in Europe knew very much, if anything at all, about Formosa and that by exploiting a situation in which he was able to pose as an authority on the subject he could, at a stroke, turn himself from a nomadic nonentity into a fantastic figure whose company would be eagerly sought after.

Psalmanazar, the name which he now took, had also realised that he had a talent for writing, an imaginative mind and a phenomenal memory. He first tried out his Formosan language on his friends in his regiment. The ruse worked and a number of officers were suitably impressed. Then, by collaborating with a Scottish chaplain, the Reverend Alexander Innes, who seems to have been in many ways a bigger and less likeable rogue than George, he went over to England to carry on his masquerade, but on a much more ambitious scale. Indeed, if one can believe George's story, as told in his *Memoirs*, posthumously published, it may well have been that Innes forced him to act as he did. It was Innes who baptised him at Sluys in 1702 just before he came to England and it could have been that Innes attempted some blackmail, if he had realised that Psalmanazar was not a Formosan.

But there is no doubt at all that, whatever his past may have been (and he always seemed intent to draw a curtain over that), George Psalmanazar wanted to succeed as a scholar. It is to his credit that when eventually he had to admit his hoax, he not only did this graciously, but from that time on set out to improve his reputation. He undertook various jobs at first, becoming a tutor in European languages, then a secretary to an Army officer, a fan-painter, at which he showed both skill and originality, and eventually returning to his former love, literature. In all these jobs he performed honestly and soberly, spending what spare time he had studying theology and Hebrew. Though ultimately he became little more than a literary hack, he produced such works as a *General History of Printing* and *Essays on Miracles*.

Perhaps his most remarkable achievement in his later years was to win the unstinted admiration of so hard a critic as Dr. Samuel Johnson himself. The doctor seems to have had a soft spot for literary forgers! What he had to say about Psalmanazar was particularly enlightening. He wrote that George's "piety, penitence and virtue exceeded almost all what we read as wonderful even in the lives of the saints". Frankly, if George had written this testimonial himself, he could hardly have bettered it.

Yet to some extent this judgement is borne out by the last will and testament of Psalmanazar, dated 1752, when he was in his seventy-third year: "The last will and testament of me, a poor simple and worthless creature, commonly known by the assumed name of George Psalmanazar". After making a devout prayer to the "Supreme Being" and directing that he might be buried in the humblest manner, he went on to say: "The principal manuscript that I felt myself bound to leave behind was a faithful narrative of my education and sallies of my wretched, youthful years, and the various ways by which I was, in some measure unadvisedly, led into the base and shameful imposture of passing upon the world for a native of Formosa and a convert to Christianity, and backing it with a fictitious account of that island and of my own travels, conversion, etc., all or most part of it hatched in my own brain, without regard to truth or honesty. It is true I have long since disclaimed even publicly all but the shame and guilt of that vile imposition, yet as long as I knew there were still two editions of that scandalous romance remaining in England, besides the several versions it had abroad, I thought it incumbent upon me to undeceive the world, by unravelling that whole mystery of iniquity in a posthumous work . . . it was no other than a mere forgery of my own devising, a scandalous imposition on the public and such as I think myself bound to beg God and the world pardon for writing."

Arthur Orton was a very different character, certainly no scholar in comparison with George Psalmanazar, but much more cunning and a resourceful actor. But where Psalmanazar was apologetic and truly anxious to admit his deception, Orton bluffed it out long after he was unmasked.

His story begins with the disappearance of Roger Charles Doughty Tichborne, son and heir of the tenth Baronet, Sir James Tichborne, member of a very old and distinguished Roman Catholic family in Britain. Sir Henry had a wife of French descent, Henriette Félicité, who not only controlled the family pursestrings by reason of her own private fortune, but because of her dominant personality. Her son Roger was educated in France before going to Stonyhurst, the Catholic public school in England. After this he served in the British Army for a spell, but seems to have been the subject of much practical joking by his fellow officers. It is recorded that on one occasion they dressed up a donkey in bonnet and shawl and placed the animal in his bed. Roger left the Army in 1852 and the following year went for a lengthy tour of South America. Before this he gave his cousin, Catherine Doughty, a document on which he had written a solemn promise to "erect a church to the Holy Virgin at Tichborne", provided he married her within three years.

In April 1854, his family received news that Roger proposed to sail for home in a ship named *Bella* on the twentieth of the month. The *Bella* duly left Rio de Janeiro on that date, but was never heard of again. An empty longboat, bearing her name, and some wreckage were found floating in the South Atlantic.

It was assumed that Roger had gone down with the ship, but Lady Tichborne refused to believe this. She insisted that her son was still alive and that one day he would be found. Nobody could convince her otherwise, though her husband did his best. She advertised for news of her son in various newspapers not only in Britain, but in foreign countries and even in Australia. In doing this she gave away a certain amount of information concerning Roger, including a description of what he looked like—"of a delicate constitution, rather tall, with very light hair and blue eyes".

Not surprisingly, these advertisements drew some strangers to the Tichborne home near Alresford in Hampshire from time to time. Some of them claimed to be survivors from the *Bella*, others just said they were sailors who had heard that Roger had been rescued. One said he was living in Patagonia on a farm, another claimed that he had heard he was in North America. Lady Tichborne not only received these strangers, but rarely let them go without providing refreshment and some money. Naturally those who told the most plausible tale and offered any hope of being able to locate Roger were given the most. Nothing, of course, was heard again from any of these strangers, but no doubt one rogue passed on the story of this lady bountiful to others, for the tactics to be repeated. The nuisance of these callers became so great that Sir James Tichborne had to arrange for some of his servants to take turns in keeping a watch in the grounds of the house to prevent strangers from reaching the gullible Lady Tichborne.

Sir James died in 1862 and it was this event alone which paved the way for someone to pose as the long-lost Roger and claim his baronetcy. What is still not altogether clear is whose idea it was originally. Almost certainly somebody of intelligence and education and a diligent reader of all manner of newspapers was the first to hit upon the idea of a carefully planned impersonation of Roger Tichborne. The various advertisements alone would supply useful information on which to base the nucleus of a plot; after that it would not have been very difficult to obtain more detailed accounts of the Tichborne family and their estates. Once news of Sir James' death had been published it would have been clear that there was no-one to protect the wishful-thinking Lady Tichborne from her fatuous convictions. As someone remarked at the time in the village of Alresford, "she was so determined to find her son that she would have identified a cow-hand as Roger if he had knocked on her door". This may have been an exaggeration, but it was not so very far from the truth.

And so in 1865 at Wagga Wagga in New South Wales, Australia, a claimant for the Tichborne baronetcy appeared on the scene. He was none other than Tom Castro, a slaughterman, supposedly of Latin American ancestry and a most improbable Roger Tichborne. Yet it is hard to believe that the idea came from Tom Castro alone. It is much more likely that the master planners of this imposture were a solicitor named Gibbes in Wagga Wagga and possibly, though to a lesser extent, a man named Cubitt in Sydney who had set up an agency for finding missing persons.

It was not unusual for advertisements to appear in the Australian press for people missing from Britain. In some cases British solicitors were seeking people who had been named as beneficiaries in wills; in others, parents seeking sons or daughters were offering rewards for news of their whereabouts. Obviously there were sufficient of these inquiries for Cubitt to make some kind of a living out of them.

But the truth about the authorship of the imposture must remain in doubt. It is largely a question of whether one regards Messrs. Gibbes and Cubitt as extremely clever or unbelievably gullible. From the day on which Tom Castro went to the solicitor Gibbes in connection with the filing of a petition for bankruptcy the idea of the impersonation was born. For Castro dropped hints to

Gibbes about estates which he had back in England, though at first he seemed loth to talk about these.

Who exactly was Tom Castro, the South American vagabond turned bushranger turned slaughterman who dropped mysterious hints to his solicitor and his cronies in Wagga Wagga that a fortune was awaiting him in England? Though nobody in Wagga Wagga appeared to know the true facts, Castro was really Arthur Orton, the son of a journey-man butcher of Wapping in London's dockland, born on March 20th, 1834, which would make him five years younger than Roger Tichborne. As a child he suffered from St. Vitus's dance after being involved in a fire. Apprenticed as a seaman, he sailed for Valparaiso in 1849 and deserted his ship as soon as he reached that port.

He made his way inland to a place named Melipilla where he won some sympathy by telling a fantastic story about his maltreatment by the captain of the ship, and that his father was butcher to Queen Victoria. For good measure he casually mentioned that he had actually played with the infant Prince of Wales! On the strength of all this, Orton was not only given free board and lodging but also funds to enable him to get back to London. True, this first effort at conmanship was practised in a primitive community, but considering that he would have had to rely on an interpreter, it was an encouraging start to a career of deception. He returned to England in 1851, worked briefly in his father's business and then sailed to Hobart in November 1852. Having been a butcher's assistant for a while, he then seemed to disappear completely.

The reason for the disappearance and his change of name to Tom Castro was undoubtedly that he had been charged with stealing a horse. Nobody ever discovered for certain what Orton did in the period immediately after his disappearance from Tasmania, but he lived and worked among bushrangers before arriving in Wagga

Wagga and ending up as a bankrupt slaughterman.

In his efforts to pose as the long-lost Roger Tichborne Orton was surprisingly subtle for one of his background. He did not come forward boldly and say "I am Sir Roger Tichborne", but modestly hinted to his mates that he came from a wealthy home in Britain, had not seen or heard from his family for many years since he was rescued from a wrecked ship in mid-Atlantic, adding that he did not like his father. It was not long before news o, these stories of Orton's reached the ears of his solicitorf Gibbes, who naturally pressed his client to tell more. At least this is what it would seem because, however much one might suspect that later Gibbes was just as much guilty of encouraging imposture, it is unlikely that he would on his own accord have selected a slaughterman with a Cockney accent to impersonate the heir to the Tichborne baronetcy.

Up to then Orton (or Castro as he claimed he was) did not mention the name Tichborne. But when he heard that Gibbes and Cubitt had taken an interest in the matter and were trying to link him with the missing Roger, he took his deception a stage further: he started to carve the initials "R.C.T." on trees, desks, and even on his pipe. After consulting together, Gibbes and Cubitt are said to have put to him the direct question: "Are you Roger Tichborne?"

Playing a game of hard-to-get, Orton reluctantly admitted that he was, but seemed highly displeased that they had guessed his secret. Within a few days he was borrowing money from Gibbes on the strength of the fact that the latter would get the "large reward" advertised for the finding of Roger Tichborne. Soon letters were speeding to England, announcing that it was believed that the Tichborne heir had been found.

The probability is that the imposture would have blown up in the face of its originator fairly speedily, but for the backing Orton received from his either very cunning or very stupid mentor, Gibbes. As Gibbes was a solicitor one must suspect that it was cunning rather than stupidity which lurked beneath the surface of his character. For when Orton first started to write to England on his own behalf he made the kind of blunders which should have stamped him as an impostor from the beginning. He spelt Roger as "Rodger" and added a "t" and a "u" to Tichborne, while he made wrong guesses at his supposed mother's Christian names.

But, stated the *True Briton* of April 25th, 1874, "the poor old lady was, however, too eager to replace her lost son to let such trifles disconcert her, and so despite of the many proofs of the fraud attempted to be practised upon her, she continued to reply to his letters and assert belief in his identity".

What Orton managed, despite his background, to do so effectively was to play on the ignorance of those in Australia about the Tichborne family and the lack of knowledge in England as to what kind of a person he was. Eventually, he wrote to Lady Tichborne in an effort to provide evidence of his identity. These few extracts will illustrate how illiterate and unconvincing the letter was:

". . . I deeply regret the truble and anxsity I must have cause you by not writing before. But they are known to my attorncy and the more private details I will keep for your own ear. Of one thing rest assured that although I have been in A humble condition of life I have never let any act disgrace you or my family. I have been a poor man and nothing worse. Mr. Gibbes suggest to me as essential That I should recall to your Memory things which can only be known to you and me to convince you of my Identity. I don't think it needful My Dear Mother. Although I send them. Namely, the Brown Mark on my side. And the Card Case at Brighton. I can assure you My Dear Mother I have kept your promise ever since. In writing to me please enclose your letter to Mr.

Gibbes to prevent unnesersery inquiry as I do not wish any person to know me in this Country . . . Having therefore made up my mind to return and face the Sea once more I must request to send me the Means of doing so paying a fue outstanding debts . . . The passage Money and other expences would be over two hundred pound. for I propose sailing from Victoria not this Colonly . . ."

Time at this stage was on Orton's side and, as the story of the sensational return of the heir to the Tichborne baronetcy was splashed across the British newspapers and especially the *Illustrated London News* with its profusion of pictures, so further snippets of information eventually arrived in Australia and were avidly seized upon by Orton to strengthen his case. These items he clipped out of newspapers and magazines and pasted them into a scrap book, the contents of which he memorised.

Lady Tichborne, despite the remonstrances of other members of her family, did not wait until she had actually seen the claimant in the flesh. She replied to his first letter by addressing Orton as "my dear son", thus acknowledging his claim before he had even left Wagga Wagga. From then on, Orton felt he had nothing to lose and that even the disadvantage of his crude habits and ungentlemanly behaviour were amply counteracted by Lady Tichborne's determination to find a son. What did his own credibility as a scion of the nobility mean compared with the near certainty that Lady Tichborne would welcome him with open arms.

On the death of Sir James Tichborne the baronetcy had passed to his second son, Alfred. Therefore, having succeeded at the first hurdle in his race for recognition, Orton faced another and more formidable hurdle in the person of the new baronet. For Sir Alfred declined to entertain even the possibility that his elder brother was still alive, was furious with his mother for consenting to see the claimant and announced that he would fight any action in the courts. Orton sailed to England, ostensibly to meet Lady Tichborne, but she was then in Paris and, instead of going straight to the French capital, Orton made his first two serious blunders: he returned incognito to Wapping to find out what had happened to his family and then paid a visit to Lloyds, the shipping agents, to make some inquiries about the *Bella*. Later, witnesses were to recall those visits and under cross-examination by the Solicitor General Orton was forced to admit them.

Perhaps recognition by Lady Tichborne had made Orton self-confident and rash because in June, 1866, before leaving for England, he had taken an appalling risk under pressure from his solicitor. The bank in Australia which had been advancing him small sums of money in anticipation of a settlement of his claims, wanted some evidence of his status. Orton obliged by making out a will in the name of Roger Tichborne. This was composed in a hurry and with scant knowledge of the Tichborne estates, so it was riddled with falsities. But Orton evidently thought that once he got to England he could make out another will and that the earlier one could be destroyed or conveniently forgotten. In this will he gave his mother's first names as Hannah Frances, which were completely wrong, leaving her property in Cowes when in fact the Tichbornes had nothing at all in the Isle of Wight.

Lady Tichborne had convinced herself that the real reason why her son had not made himself known long before was that after his ordeal at sea he had suffered from a loss of memory and that to some extent he was still affected by this. All this, of course, played right into Orton's hands, for, when baffled by questions from those who interrogated him in England, he was able to plead forgetfulness.

When eventually he went to Paris he feigned illness on

his first meeting with Lady Tichborne, taking to his bed and begging her to come and see him. She did so, announced immediately that she recognised her son and that until he got back his estates she would allow him a thousand pounds a year. From then on anyone in her service who disputed Orton's claim to be Roger Tichborne was instantly dismissed. Her own solicitor was sent packing for merely urging caution and suggesting that some further proofs were needed.

In some respects, Orton showed a genius for organisation in his gigantic imposture. He set out to provide himself with not just a few, but literally scores of witnesses and supporters to his claims. Many of these were unscrupulous rogues who were anxious to take the bribes which he was now in a position to offer them. But others were bluffed into lending him their support. The most valuable supporter of his cause was a man named Bogle who had been in service with the Tichbornes almost all his life. In one of the letters which Lady Tichborne had written to Orton before he left Australia she mentioned that Bogle was now living in Sydney. This was too good a chance to miss. Orton went to see Bogle, by then an old man, and swiftly convinced him that he was indeed Roger Tichborne. Naturally, Orton had taken the precaution of having Bogle pointed out to him beforehand and then went up to the man and pretended to recognise him. Bogle agreed to accompany Orton to England and to support his claim with evidence. No doubt during the voyage Orton obtained an enormous amount of valuable information about the Tichbornes and their friends by cleverly questioning the unsuspecting Bogle.

At the suggestion of a number of cunning rogues, a company was formed and Tichborne Bonds were issued in anticipation of the acceptance of Orton's claim. As the printing of these bonds cost little, they were given away to many people, one newspaper proprietor receiving a bribe to lend his support. Fools bought the Bonds, rascals obtained them without paying. Thus many people became interested in the claimant's success.

The Tichborne Case, as it became known, is still the longest trial in the annals of British justice. The civil trial, in which Orton pressed his claim, began on May 11th, 1872, and lasted 103 days until the claimant's case collapsed completely. The criminal trial, which followed, lasted 188 days, ending in Orton being found guilty of perjury and sentenced to fourteen years' imprisonment and hard labour. The case was reported to have cost £55,315, which in terms of today's costs would be the equivalent of half a million. This cost the Tichborne estate a considerable sum.

What was most remarkable about this whole affair was how it aroused fierce partisanship and enmity between rival bands of supporters across the whole of England. No other case in the whole of British history has caused such tremendous controversy among the general public. It saw the publication of a new broadsheet, *The True Briton] The Avowed Enemy and Antidote to Dr. Kenealy's 'Englishman'*, which was part of the anti-Orton campaign, Dr. Kenealy being Orton's counsel and the editor of *The Englishman.* Those who supported Orton launched the Tichborne Defence Fund and raised money for this by pigeon-shooting matches. Politics entered into it when many Tories backed the real baronet and left-wing Radicals were persuaded that there was a right-wing Establishment plot to thwart the claimant. Protestants attacked the claimant and his supporters as being "part of a Jesuit conspiracy", one letter-writer to the press complaining that the "claimant's chief supporters were among the Roman Catholics themselves".

There is a curious footnote to this story. An ancient charity maintained by the Tichborne family was said to have been started by Lady Mabel Tichborne in 1150. She is said to have begged her husband to provide for the poor from the produce of the estate and to have declared that if the charity were allowed to lapse, seven sons would be born to the family followed by seven daughters, after which the title would lapse. After 644 years the charity was stopped and the then baronet had seven sons and his heir seven daughters. The third son changed his name to Doughty, revived the charity and escaped the full consequences of the curse. The title became extinct with the death of Sir Anthony Doughty-Tichborne in 1968.

Was Lady Tichborne conscious of this curse and did she believe that by supporting the claimant she would preserve the line because he would not be directly involved? Was she anxious to found a line of her own—a puppet Tichborne in the person of Orton who could wreak revenge against the real Tichborne family, most of whom she detested? There is ample evidence that not only was she on the worst possible terms with her son, the real baronet, but that her missing son, Roger, had broken with her before he sailed for South America. She was a Frenchwoman and, above all else, an Anglophobe. It is not beyond the realms of possibility that she knew perfectly well that Orton was not Roger, but that she stubbornly persisted in the charade in order to irritate and ruin the Tichbornes. Indeed, one might even carry speculation into the sphere of fantasy and say that it is not improbable that Orton may have been one of the strangers claiming to know what happened to the *Bella*, calling on her before he went to Australia. She continued to give him twenty pounds a week until her sudden death in 1868. It was after this that Orton was forced to launch the Tichborne Bonds to be repaid at a high premium after he had recovered his estates.

All that is certain is that without Lady Tichborne this whole costly, farcical impersonation and the lengthy court case would not have been possible. When Orton lost his "mother" he lost the case.

10

PRACTICAL JOKER WHO PLANNED HIS OWN "DEATH"

THERE HAVE been confidence tricksters intent only on monetary rewards, or furthering their careers; there have been others who delighted in impersonation for its own sake, or simply in exploiting their skills. But Clarence Adams was in a class by himself. He revelled in a bizarre form of practical joking which culminated in his conning his fellow citizens into believing he was dead.

Many practical jokers just fail to come within the fairly broad definition of con-tricksters which has been set out in this book. But Adams certainly deserved to be included in this company, if only for his persistence and the quirks in his character which prompted his macabre exploits.

The motivation for Adams' unique brand of conmanship was his love of books on crime, the occult, mystery and detective stories. Not only did he collect such books himself, but as chief trustee of the public library of the town of Chester in Windsor County, New England, he carefully selected such works for its readers. To the undiscerning, Adams was merely a wealthy man indulging a taste for book collecting and for enabling others to borrow what he could afford to buy. But in the privacy of his home, a farm-house on the outskirts of

Chester, he could have been found browsing for hours in his private library, living in a world of fantasy among the works of Poe (his great favourite), Hoffmann, Wilkie Collins and Stevenson.

It is not exaggerating to say that this hobby of Adams became an obsession which dominated his private and indeed his secret life. He would read and re-read these books, sometimes copying out whole passages and making notes, at others sitting back with eyes closed, apparently in a deep reverie.

In public he appeared as an energetic, altruistic farmer and spokesman in local government, having served as a member of the legislature for several years. He had inherited property and was a man of substantial means.

One of Adams' favourite authors was Robert Louis Stevenson, who he was said to have met during that author's visit to New York. Of all Stevenson's works the one which most appealed to Adams was the horrific *Dr. Jekyll and Mr. Hyde*, published in 1886. It was this work, said to have been inspired by a dream which Stevenson had, which turned Adams' mind towards the idea of conning his fellow citizens. Adams wanted to see if he could succeed where Dr. Jekyll ultimately failed, that is by creating a fool-proof double life.

So in about 1886 the secretive Adams began to play the role of Mr. Hyde, though not quite in the same way. Adams became a burglar who set off at night systematically to rob neighbours, factories and warehouses, not because he needed the money, but to test out his theory that it was possible to lead a double life successfully and to fool a whole community. There he was, presiding over committee meetings, acting as a welfare officer to keep an eye on juvenile delinquents, tending to his farm and, of course, spending a good deal of time in the public library. He had no family to worry about and he had carefully chosen for his housekeeper an old woman who did as she was told and asked no questions. While in the library Adams did rather more than supervise the staff and select books; he built up a collection of technical reference books on a wide range of subjects intended to enable him to live a double life. In particular, he made copious notes on various criminal cases in New York and New England which were listed in some detail in the library files. Above all, he studied where the criminals had made fatal mistakes.

For something like sixteen years Adams conducted a brilliantly planned series of burglaries, almost invariably during the night hours. Nobody was ever sure as to the full extent of his crimes, but they ranged from robberies of clothes, jewellery, cash and a wide range of goods from shops to even grain from warehouses and paintings and silver from private houses. The robberies baffled the police who were blamed for slackness. Clarence Adams himself was among those who criticised the police at public meetings, even putting forward his own theories as to the type of person they should be looking for. At first, it was suspected that the Chester area was being subjected to these crimes by a gang and a number of arrests of known burglars were made.

One day in 1902 a doctor was summoned urgently to Adams' home and then the truth was out, for Adams had been seriously wounded by a spring-gun which had been set in an effort to trap the mysterious burglar at a local mill. There was no opportunity for him to deny having been at the mill, because traces of his blood had been discovered there.

Some of the objects he had stolen were recovered, but a very great deal had been safely hidden away out of reach of the local police. Even when facing sentence, Adams gave nothing away. All he would say was: "It has all been a great adventure and I have had a lot of enjoyment out of it. Being a burglar has kept me mentally alert all these years and I have proved to myself that, if studied properly, like a profession, it can be carried out despite all the police in the world. But I never did this for money, only for the sheer fun of it."

He was sent to the State Prison at Windsor to serve ten years. Not surprisingly, he was a model prisoner, though regarded as somewhat of a lunatic. Nothing could have been further from the truth and the prison authorities must have wished that they had treated Adams rather differently than as a harmless eccentric. Because of his education and the fact that he was a cut above most of the prisoners, Adams was given relatively congenial tasks, being put in charge of the library and asked to give some of the prisoners lessons in various subjects.

With this degree of freedom and the knowledge that he was not under the strictest surveillance, Adams began to plan his biggest con trick of all. It was so coolly, so lucidly and successfully planned that one almost wonders whether being arrested by the police and sent to prison was not part of his scheme. Did he tire of not getting caught after so many years of burglary? Was the planning of his escape and creating the impression that he was dead his final thrill? And were the proceeds of all those robberies turned into funds which were stacked away in bank accounts at far distant places under another name?

The answer to all these queries is almost certainly that Adams was not only clever and eccentric enough to prepare the ground for such a macabre escape from prison, but that he had thought up the whole project long before he was arrested. Adams was no ordinary con-man: he plotted for every eventuality years ahead, and as his hoaxing of the community in which he lived was his sole recreation, he was able to spend a great deal of time thinking out every detail to its logical conclusion. He must have decided that sooner or later the law of averages decreed that he would be caught and that there could be no future for him in Chester after his release from prison. So he determined that he must appear to be dead and then take on a new identity.

One of his first steps was to study hypnosis and especially self-induced hypnosis. He ordered books touching on this subject for the Chester Library and paid particular attention to the works of Charcot and Pierre Janet. Then, having absorbed and memorised this information, he learned within a few months how to induce in himself a condition of suspended animation, largely done by verbal suggestion, bringing about the kind of changes in pulse rate and apparent paralysis of some muscles which would indicate the approach of death and which, in some circumstances, could suggest the condition of death itself. He continued to practice self-hypnosis inside prison.

Before Adams went to prison he had ensured that he had outside help. He had actually employed a few professional burglars to help carry out some of his raids in the vicinity of Chester, and, as he was not greedy for loot, and as he could also advise them on tactics, he retained their loyalty. But even then he was wise enough to make allowance for the probability of human frailty, for he managed to smuggle into jail several thousands of dollars and this was the bait he promised, if they would assist him in his escape. His main confederate in prison was a convict who had been a doctor.

Not a single detail seems to have been missed in Adams' planning of his faked death and escape. He knew that, while summer was the ideal time to make an escape from the viewpoint of warmth and comfort for the single night in which he might have to stay in the vault of a cemetery, that nevertheless a faked death in winter would be far less hazardous. For Adams had decided exactly where he intended to be "buried" and had named this place in his will, as well as the person who was to collect his body from the prison. Indeed, it was

Adams' will which clinches the evidence that this was a long-term plot. He had chosen for his burial place a small cemetery at a lonely site known as Cavendish some distance away from Chester. It was an ideal situation for rescuing a body at night-time. But it had one overall advantage. In summer-time, when the weather was hot, it was the custom for bodies to be buried immediately at Cavendish. But in the winter months the ground here was permanently so hard with frost that digging was difficult. It was, therefore, the invariable custom for coffins to be left in the cemetery vault until spring before they were taken out and buried.

So "death" was planned for the time when frosts were most severe in the area, the month of February, 1904. Years later an old lag told how Adams had even managed to consult meterorological experts in prison and that on George Washington's birthday anniversary that year he had been told that the forecast was for a spell of extreme cold. At any rate, on this day he complained of feeling ill and was admitted to the prison hospital. As his condition did not seem serious enough to warrant calling in an outside doctor, the services of the convict doctor were utilised. On February 26th this same doctor announced that Adams was dead and he signed a death certificate stating that the cause of death was pneumonia. There was apparently an appalling slackness in prison regulations on such matters, presumably to keep down costs. The convict doctor's certificate was simply sent on to the visiting doctor who counter-signed it without having examined the allegedly dead man. It is true that the prison governor had paid a swift visit to the mortuary to confirm that he really was dead, but Adams had trained himself to breathe almost imperceptibly while in a trance and with cotton-wool stuffed in his nostrils by the convict doctor, it was not difficult to deceive a layman who only flicked aside the sheets to give a cursory examination.

The man named in Adams' will—William Dunn—promptly arrived to collect the body with the full authority of an undertaker. He arrived with a coffin, lined with wool and with concealed air holes. Adams was carried into his undertaker's van and taken to Cavendish. Here the coffin was locked up in the vault to await burial in the spring.

Adams did not have to spend many hours in this chilly vault. His fellow-conspirators arrived in the night, opened up the vault, removed the coffin and released Adams who was plied with spirits and given warm clothing. The locks were put back on the door to the vault so that nobody would detect the intrusion. Adams was taken to a distant town where he was supplied with a disguise and eventually he made his way across the border into Canada.

But Adams' confidence trick was not yet finished. Anyone who had planned as carefully as this could have got away with the whole hoax completely, if he had wished. But some writers on the Adams story have suggested that he was careless and swiftly discovered in Nova Scotia. It is true that some few months after his supposed death someone returning to Chester claimed to have seen him in Nova Scotia. As a result, the cemetery vault was inspected and the top of the coffin removed. Sure enough there was a body inside it, though decomposition prevented the authorities from absolutely identifying the corpse as that of Adams. A post mortem and a thorough examination could have told more, but it was assumed from this cursory inspection that all was well. Later the coffin was buried. A year afterwards, other reports came through that Adams had been seen and, so some people said, actually spoken to. There was a demand for an official inquiry into whether or not he had been buried.

Somehow the authorities managed to avoid carrying out such an inquiry. Rumour had it that Adams had even prevented this and that his power of silencing individuals was effective even from his self-imposed exile. Much later it was reported that he had left Canada and gone to Mexico. It is more likely that Adams could not resist letting the people of Chester know he had hoaxed them and that he was still alive. So, when his first attempt to give them this news was not accepted, he had to make himself known personally on the second occasion.

In any event, he was never heard of again. Maybe he remained in Canada, or even went to Europe. Most probably the story of his going to Mexico was simply a rumour he himself planted to mislead people. For he was never heard of again except for once in 1911 when the librarian at Chester received a mysterious postcard from Paris. It was posted on February 26th, the anniversary of Adams' "death" and in printed letters were the words "In memory of Clarence Adams, the immortal joker. R.I.P."

11

THE POLICE AGENT WHO STAGED MURDERS

IEVNO AZEFF will certainly go down in history as the one double-agent nobody completely unmasked. For that reason alone he deserves a place among the aces of conmanship.

It is, of course, part and parcel of the career of a double-agent, or indeed of an ordinary skilled agent to pretend to be what he is not. The tactics of the *agent provocateur* are recognised weapons in the armoury both of a secret agent and a member of the criminal investigation sections of police in many countries. But Ievno Azeff went far beyond such incidental techniques. He not only posed as a revolutionary while working for the police as an informer and secret agent, but actually organised assassinations of leading political figures in Russia so that he could trap the killers and their associates into being arrested and executed.

Indeed, for every blow he struck against the revolutionaries, he seemed to hit back equally hard against the police. No-one was more adept at tracking down and enabling the police to arrest key revolutionary figures and at the same time more skilled in advancing the revolutionary cause with some spectacular coup. Which side obtained most benefit? It is almost impossible to say, but what is certain is that Azeff himself made a fortune out of conning both sides.

"So skilfully did he conceal his tracks," writes Graham Stephenson, the modern British authority on Russian history, "that it is impossible to say which side he mainly betrayed." Long after he had ceased to operate in the devious world of underground revolutionaries and the Czarist secret police, Azeff continued to disconcert those in authority. A. T. Vassilyev, who was chief of the Ochrana, the Czar's secret police, had to admit that, in his own words, "no clear light has ever been shed on the Azeff affair. Nor did I, during my whole period of service ever set eyes upon any documents that might have been likely to clear up that mysterious business."

Ievno Azeff was the son of a poor Jewish tailor, born in 1869 at Lyskovo in the Grodnensky province of Russia. Later the family moved to Rostov and young Azeff took various jobs for brief periods, first as a clerk, then as a tutor and, finally as reporter on a small newspaper. He made friends with a number of revolutionaries and, when he had to escape from Russia after being wanted for absconding with a sum of money, joined the Russian Democratic Group in Exile in Karlsruhe, Germany.

This gave him the idea of making some money and winning his way back to favour in Russia by betraying the group to the police. So in 1893 Azeff started his career as a police informer by sending a letter to the Ochrana, giving them an account of the Group's activities together with the names of members. He gave a false name when writing to them. Eventually he received a reply that was non-commital, but called Azeff's bluff. It indicated that if he would reveal his real name and exactly where he could be reached, he would be paid.

This was a start, but Azeff was equally cautious. Though he replied by return, he still did not reveal his real name. The Ochrana, however, made inquiries on their own account and managed through their own agents to establish his real identity. A year later he was employed on a trial basis as one of their agents abroad.

Immediately Azeff thew himself wholeheartedly into revolutionary circles. Deliberately, so that he could obtain information on the more dangerous of the Russian exiles, he posed as an extremist, urging the use of terrorist tactics. Soon he became a back-room agitator, prominent in the secret councils of the revolutionary movement.

From all accounts he was not a particularly prepossessing character. One contemporary account describes him as being "ugly, with a puffy, yellow face, a simian nose and thick lips". Yet he seems to have won the confidence of both the secret police and his fellow revolutionaries in a remarkably short time. For Azeff worked hard and produced results. As he was being paid by the Ochrana, he could afford to give longer hours to revolutionary business than most of his comrades. This gave him a reputation for being dedicated. As he spent so much time in revolutionary circles, travelling around from one foreign centre to another, he was able to send the police lengthy reports.

In 1899 his salary was doubled and it was suggested that he should return to Russia. He had obtained the diploma of an electrical engineer and the Ochrana promised they would not only increase his salary further, but also find him a post as an engineer. So he went to Moscow and established links with other revolutionary organisations. It was through Azeff's information that the Czarist police were able to raid a subversive printing works in Tomsk and round up a number of terrorist leaders. And just to prove what a master of conmanship he was, when all the leaders of this terrorist group were arrested, Azeff got himself elected leader of the whole organisation. By this means he learned all the inner workings of the high command of the revolutionaries and their various cells outside as well as inside Russia.

By the turn of the century Azeff was earning five hundred roubles a month from the Ochrana, possibly the highest rate of pay for any of their secret agents. He had enabled them to penetrate the innermost circles of the Social Revolutionaries' movement. More important still he had informed the police of the setting up of a special squad of the revolutionaries known as the "Battle Organisation", whose aim was the assassination of top Russian statesmen.

Azeff even gave the Ochrana the name of the top man in this secret section. G. A. Gershuni, but insisted that on no account must Gershuni be arrested yet, as such an action would inevitably mean that he would be suspected of betraying the organisation.

Meanwhile Azeff urged the "Battle Organisation" to boost the revolutionary cause by killing off leading supporters of the Czar's Government. In April, 1902, Sipyagin, the Minister of the Interior, was assassinated. Though Azeff, then in Berlin, sent in a stream of valuable reports to police headquarters, he went out of his way to inform them that Gershuni was not connected with the assassination. Only when Gershuni actually left Russia did Azeff reveal that Gershuni was involved in the killing.

About this time Azeff started to pass back to the revolutionaries information he gained from his police contacts. The Ochrana believed that Azeff's position in the party was dependent on his friendship with Gershuni. It would seem that more than once Azeff was about to betray Gershuni, but that he always hesitated at the last moment. There was perhaps a clue in one extremely candid message which Azeff sent to the Police Department when he reported a dynamite factory which the revolutionaries had set up in Switzerland: "My position has become somewhat dangerous. I am now playing a very active part among revolutionaries. It would be unprofitable to retreat now, but any action calls for the greatest care."

In this tangled web of his own weaving this adroit police agent operated with cunning, skill and astute judgement. He revealed to the Ochrana Gershuni's plans for killing W. K. Plehve, the new Minister of the Interior, and Zubatoff, head of the Moscow branch of the Ochrana, but he kept silent on the target for the next killing—that of Obolensky, Governor of Kharkov. His tactics were to safeguard all his supporters within the revolutionary movement, but to eliminate his enemies and those suspicious of him by giving them away to the police. Later, the Petersburg Social Revolutionary Committee came completely under Azeff's direction. He also formed several new branches of the movement, quite often manning them with Ochrana agents.

For a while the revolutionaries seemed to be entirely satisfied with Azeff, but inside the Ochrana doubts about their top agent were expressed. He was pressed to provide information which would lead to the arrest of Gershuni. The Czar had secretly offered a reward of 15,000 roubles for Gershuni's capture, and Azeff was obviously tempted to make a deal for he made a counter-offer, asking for 50,000 roubles and an assurance that no matter who arrested Gershuni he alone would get the money. Not surprisingly the Ochrana were somewhat dubious about this proposal.

Shortly afterwards Azeff met Gershuni secretly in Moscow and it is almost certain that they discussed plans for killing Bodganovitch, Governor of Ufa. Immediately after this meeting Gershuni went to Ufa and Bodganovitch was shot by terrorists.

But Gershuni was arrested a few months later and it was then that Azeff acquired supreme command of the revolutionary group and directed terrorist tactics. As the chief of the "Battle Organisation" he had large sums of money under his control. There is abundant evidence in the files of the Ochrana that he obtained sums of money for himself both from police and revolutionary funds.

In the case of the next victim of the terrorists it is possible that Azeff had a personal reason for wanting to see him dead. For the next on the list to be assassinated was Plehve, the much hated Minister of the Interior. Azeff believed that Plehve was an instigator of persecution of the Jewish communities in Russia. Thus he organised this assassination personally, taking the utmost precautions against discovery by the police and even eliminating a rival group of terrorists who had also planned to kill Plehve. The latter incident was a bonus for Azeff. A fanatical woman terrorist, S. Klitchoglu, had founded her own group of assassins. Azeff lost no time in revealing her plans to kill Plehve to the Ochrana, thus gaining their confidence at a time when he was somewhat under a cloud and also eliminating a rival. Perhaps the removal of Klitchoglu was all-important because some of the revolutionaries were impatient with Azeff for his extreme caution in pursuing the plan to kill the Minister of the Interior. More than once Azeff had called off an assassination attempt on Plehve.

But Klitchoglu was arrested and then on July 18th, 1904, Plehve was killed when a bomb was hurled at his carriage. The Ochrana, who had long expected an attempt on the Minister's life, were highly suspicious that they had had no tip-off from Azeff, for they must have guessed that their own agent was now head of the "Battle Organisation". Prudently, their ace agent had managed to move to Vienna at this time and from there he had the cool impertinence to inform the Ochrana that "Plehve's assassination was a complete surprise to me."

Before the secret police had recovered from the Plehve killing they were confronted with yet another crime—

the murder of the Grand Duke Sergei Alexandrovitch. It was then whispered that the Czar himself was next on the list. Later, in his memoirs, the then Prime Minister of Russia, Count Witte, expressed the belief that "the Grand Duke was killed on direct orders from Azeff, the police agent". Yet Witte himself took no steps at the time to act against Azeff, or to try and reverse the *agent provocateur* tactics which the Ochrana were indulging in.

But in due course changes in the direction of the secret police rebounded against Azeff. He was soon made to realise that unless he could come up with some really sensational information, his days with the Ochrana were numbered. Yet curiously, perhaps in an effort to lull him into a false sense of security, Ratchkovsky, the new chief of Azeff's department in the Ochrana, increased his salary to 600 roubles and even allowed him to draw the sum of 1,300 roubles for expenses. But, unknown to Azeff, the revolutionaries had managed to infiltrate the ranks of the Ochrana and one of them, L. P. Menstchikoff, discovered that Azeff was a police agent and was, as he reported back, "systematically betraying the party".

Such was Azeff's authority and standing within the revolutionary movement that this report was not only disbelieved, but not even made the subject of an inquiry. During this period Azeff was earning more than 16,000 roubles a year from the secret police. Sometime after this he temporarily retired to live a life of ease and luxury on the Italian Riviera, but was recalled with an offer of even more money to tackle the ever-growing problem of the terrorists.

Though he uncovered a new ally of the terrorists in the person of a retired Russian naval lieutenant and through this caused the arrest of twenty-eight revolutionaries, Savinkov, one of the terrorist leaders had such confidence in him at the time to say: "I should not have believed in his guilt even if I had seen it stated in his own handwriting. I should have considered that a forgery".

However, a few in the revolutionary ranks had their doubts about Azeff. One of them set out on his own to obtain evidence against the unidentified traitor within their movement. This was V. L. Burtsev, an academic revolutionary who took life very seriously. Not only were his warnings against Azeff ignored, but Burtsev was ordered by the Central Revolutionary Committee to be "tried" for libelling Azeff. This so-called trial took place in what the revolutionaries called their "Court of Honour" in Paris.

At this trial one revolutionary after another testified to Azeff's achievements for "the cause". At the end, Savinkov, who was one of the prosecutors, asked Burtsev: "Now that we have told you of Azeff's achievements, can you tell us whether there exists in the history of the Russian revolutionary movement a more brilliant name than that of Azeff?"

Finally, Burtsev was brutally told by the president of the court: "If your accusations are proved groundless, you will have nothing else to do but shoot yourself for all the harm you have done to the Revolution".

Then Burtsev revealed certain facts about Azeff that he had been given by a former chief of the Czarist police. This probably saved Burtsev's life, but it marked the beginning of the end for Azeff. Burtsev was partially exonerated with the stipulation that there must be a further investigation of Azeff's conduct.

Perhaps Azeff had begun to believe that his position as a double-agent was impregnable. In one sense it was relatively fool-proof, because Azeff, unlike most double-agents, had allowed each side to know that to some extent he worked in with the other. He had always convinced each side that it was the other who had been double-crossed. At the same time, Azeff was tipping off the Ochrana that the funds of the Central Committee of the revolutionaries were being boosted to the extent of 300,000 roubles through a raid on the Charjui Government treasury. The secret police chief, Gerassimov, who received this information, did not ask Azeff to arrange for this money to be captured by the Ochrana, despite the fact that the Russian Prime Minister had given orders that the raiders should be arrested and the money restored to the authorities. As far as Gerassimov was concerned, he was quite content to allow Azeff to obtain for himself a major share of this money on the tacit understanding that he did not ask for a rise in his police salary. So Azeff arranged for the money to be transferred to Turkestan and collected his share there.

Just how security-minded Azeff was may be gathered from the fact that his wife was a fanatical, idealistic revolutionary who would almost certainly have denounced her husband if she had had any inkling of his role with the Ochrana. But she never guessed and Azeff found consolation from time to time with a German cabaret singer he had met in St. Petersburg.

As the net tightened around Azeff so he planned even more daring coups to restore the confidence of the revolutionaries in his devotion to their cause. He decided that if he could successfully arrange the assassination of the Czar nobody could possibly believe he was an Ochrana agent. A new Russian cruiser, the *Rurik*, was being built at Glasgow and was to sail to Russia to be inspected by the Czar. Azeff went to Glasgow to make plans for the assassination attempt. He had selected a member of the crew named Avdeyev, a dedicated secret revolutionary, as the assassin. Giving this sailor a revolver and detailed instructions, Azeff cunningly persuaded the man to write him a letter explaining his motives for his action, on the understanding that this would be published after the attempt on the Czar's life had been made.

Azeff's plan for himself was simple but inspired and, if it came off, he would emerge with even greater authority than ever. He was to return to his apartment in Paris—all these years he had maintained establishments of his own in most of the big capitals of Europe—and there await a telegram telling him that the Czar had been killed. Then, with Avdeyev's letter in his possession, he could finally confront his revolutionary critics with proof of his fidelity.

But the attempt on the Czar was never made and from then on Azeff was doomed. The revolutionaries sent a delegation to cross-examine him in Paris, but he left his apartment in the middle of the night, taking care to put the Avdeyev letter in a prominent position on his desk. January, 1909, marked the end of Azeff's career both as a revolutionary and as an Ochrana agent. He disappeared to Germany with his mistress.

There was uproar in St. Petersburg and a number of heads rolled in the upper echelons of the secret police. It is doubtful if the Ochrana ever recovered from what eventually became known as the "Azeff Affair". As for Azeff himself, not even his riches gave him much security. He kept on the move, always dreading an attempt on his life by the Ochrana or the revolutionaries. He visited Italy, Greece and Egypt, changing his name and his hotel every few weeks. With the advent of World War I, Azeff's life of luxury and comfort also came to an end. He had changed his name to Alexander Neumayer, but the German secret police discovered his true identity. They arrested him not because he had been an agent of the Ochrana, but because he was looked upon as a dangerous revolutionary. Somehow, whether because he lost his nerve, or his mistress spent too much of his money, or the effects of the war, he lost his fortune. So not even the resourceful Ievno Azeff was able to buy his way out of a German prison.

In 1917 he was released from prison. Perhaps the Germans, who had come to terms with the Russian revolutionaries, thought Azeff could be an ally. But by then his spirit was broken. He went to live in Berlin and there he died on April 24th, 1918.

What might have happened if he had managed to get the Czar killed in 1908 is a fascinating subject for speculation. He could have become an outstanding leader of the revolution and, if he had at the same time risen still higher in the ranks of the Ochrana, he could eventually have become first head of the Soviet Secret Service. Yet somehow I imagine that Ievno Azeff was always too much of an individualist to devote himself to any one side.

12

THE GREATEST CRAFTSMAN OF THEM ALL

IT WILL long remain one of the great psychological mysteries of the art world how it was that a man like Hans Van Meegeren, whose own original paintings won him only meagre recognition in his lifetime, could show such brilliant craftsmanship in copying the works of a great master and fool some of the greatest art experts of his day.

But it was to establish his talent in his own mind, if not in that of the general public, that Van Meegeren carried out his confidence trick with superb aplomb, great pertinacity, at no little risk and, above all, with a total contempt for most art critics. What is more, he maintained the imposture from at least 1936 until the end of World War II. Even when he was finally declared to be a trickster, Van Meegeren could claim that at least his chicanery was directed more against his country's enemies than anyone else, not to mention the fact that it was he who confessed to the hoax and that at first the art experts refused to believe him.

Hans Van Meegeren was born in 1889. As a child his health was not too good and this, coupled with his small stature, made him feel the odd one out at school. Possibly because he felt he had obstacles to overcome, he became obsessed with achieving success. But this obsession he kept to himself and silently plotted his own lone path to secret fame. Unknown to many people, Van Meegeren studied painting and practised copying the works of the great masters as a youth while he was taking a course in architecture at the Institute of Technology at Delft in Holland.

Delft was also the birthplace of the great Dutch portrait painter, Johannes Vermeer (1632-75) and it was this artist who the young van Meegeren studied in depth, spending long hours just looking at Vermeer paintings in different lights, taking copious notes of exactly how they appeared at sunset, at high noon and in early morning, as well as under artificial light. Unquestionably, Van Meegeren became an authority on Vermeer, but this was something he did not flaunt.

However, he did switch his attention permanently from architecture to painting, and shortly before World War I he married and took up a post as a teacher of drawing and art history in Delft. In his spare time he did a certain amount of painting on his own account, but he found great difficulty in making much money out of this, even though he won a number of prizes for his work. Slowly it dawned on him that the kind of subjects he liked painting were of no interest to the picture-buying public in Holland. On the other hand, when he painted what they did like, the critics attacked his work as being "mundane" or "unimaginative". His craftsmanship was overlooked. In other words, here was a skilled painter with brilliant techniques, yet one who could win over neither the public nor the critics.

There was no inferiority complex about Van Meegeren. He knew that he was a great craftsman and that, when it came to the test, he was far superior to many highly successful contemporary painters. He also knew that, far from being mundane when he painted what he really liked, his work was imaginative, original, even bizarre. In fact, it was too bizarre for the public and the critics. He painted pictures of dainty roebucks sniffing almond blossom and of Paderewski-style pianists receiving inspiration from the ghost of Liszt. Some said there was the smell of brimstone and black magic about his pictures.

In the beginning the sole motive Van Meegeren had for embarking on a career of forgery—the forging of works by one of Holland's favourite great masters—was to revenge himself upon the art critics. His idea was to paint one Vermeer picture and then, when it had been acknowledged as genuine and praised by the critics, to reveal that it was a practical joke aimed at showing up those who claimed to be the arbiters of great painting. Years afterwards Van Meegeren's daughter said: "Beyond doubt he was a good painter. When he was quite a young man he won a gold medal in a big Dutch competition. Holland is a very small country and the competition between artists is intense. If you did not bribe a critic, then you got a bad notice. They could make or murder you. My father set out to prove that the critics were fools."

In choosing Vermeer for the subject of his exercise in forgery, Van Meegeren was influenced by the fact that he had made such a great study of this artist and that he knew probably more than most about Vermeer's life and career. There was the added advantage for a forger that Vermeer pictures, which ranged from portraits to genre scenes and landscape and town views, were comparatively rare and therefore costly. Many of his works were known to have disappeared completely. Maybe, too, there was the feeling that Vermeer himself, like Van Meegeren, had been badly treated by many art critics and ignored for at least two centuries after his death.

Certainly, no forger ever paid such attention to detail as Van Meegeren. The fact that he was a skilled craftsman who could turn out superb copies of Vermeer's own work, which he greatly admired, was not enough. He had to create pictures which would pass for works of the seventeenth century. Van Meegeren made several attempts to copy just one Vermeer before he was satisfied. Then he set out to comb the country for the exact materials which Vermeer would have used. He knew that only the most meticulous forgery would fool the critics. So he bought old canvases and removed the paint from them with pumice stone and water. He obtained the raw materials to manufacture his pigments just as Vermeer had done, because today virtually all pigments are synthetic and may be identified.

All this preparatory work is said to have taken Van Meegeren fifteen years. In the old days, painters possessed but one solid colour, the blue of lapis lazuli, which was used by all the great masters. This was eventually replaced by ultramarine and lapis lazuli became so scarce that its price soared to fantastic heights. Van Meegeren is reputed to have paid a sum in excess of one hundred pounds for a small quantity of lapis lazuli.

The subject he first chose to forge under the initials of Vermeer, which, ironically, were the same as his own, was that of Christ and his Disciples at Emmaus, which became known as *De Emmausganger*. Van Meegeren was clever enough not to paint this in Vermeer's well known and mature Dutch style, but in a hypothetical, earlier Italianate manner, somewhat like Caravaggio seen through Dutch eyes.

It was in 1936 that the painter from Delft produced his *De Emmausganger*. He said that he discovered and "recognised" this work hidden away in a cupboard in Paris. Approaching one of Holland's greatest art experts, telling him he had bought the picture cheaply, Van Meegeren obtained a certificate of authenticity that this was indeed a Vermeer. Indeed, the enthusiastic art critic and historian, Dr. Abraham Bredius, said of the work: "we have here *the* masterpiece of Johannes

Vermeer, and, moreover, one of his largest works, quite different from all his other paintings and yet every inch a Vermeer."

Armed with this testimony, Van Meegeren sold his fake to the Boyman's Museum in Rotterdam in 1937 for the sum of £62,000. The millionaire benefactor of this museum, D. G. van Beuningen, provided the cash.

For a while Van Meegeren went to live at a villa in the South of France. Some say that his original intention had been to play this trick on the critics and then, in triumph, to admit that he had painted the picture himself and to have torn up the cheque paid to him. Thus he would vindicate himself and throw the critics into confusion. But, apart from the fact that the temptation of so much money so easily earned must have been great, there is the equal probability that Van Meegeren began to realise that nobody would believe him if he confessed.

So he continued to forge Vermeers. For his second fake Vermeer, "Anointment of the Feet", he was paid £125,000. A third picture, a small study of Christ's head, went for £40,000. But it was the advent of World War II which provided Van Meegeren with the ideal conditions under which to operate. The Dutch Government forbade the export of great Dutch paintings from Holland, so Van Meegeren's forgeries were smuggled out of the country in the utmost secrecy and sold to such avid German collectors of works of art as Hermann Goering. Already rich, Van Meegeren now cynically proceeded to fleece wealthy Nazi patrons of the arts of their ill-gotten gains. Most of these transactions took place while Holland was occupied by the Germans. Van Meegeren established secret links of communication with a German banker named Miedl who had taken over an art gallery in Amsterdam.

So we have the amusing black comedy of the Dutch forger finding an anonymous, allegedly impoverished family as the go-between to sell to Miedl and through the banker to Goering himself yet another precious Vermeer, this time a work called "Christ and the Adulteress". The price Goering paid for this was £150,000.

During the war he painted five more Vermeers and two fakes of Pieter de Hoochs, a contemporary of Vermeer. It has been said that Van Meegeren made the best part of a million pounds out of these fakes. He carried out most of his work in a locked room which nobody, not even his wife, was allowed to enter. Even then he had to persuade his wife to go out for a whole day on those occasions when he "baked" his canvases to give the impression of age. In actually selling his pictures in these war years he conducted operations like a master spy, using a lawyer as intermediary and getting this man always to spin the story of the anonymous family who had fallen on hard times and needed to sell their most precious possessions.

It has sometimes been said that Van Meegeren was a man of deplorable taste in decorating his home. Yet it is much more likely that this so-called poor taste was simply intended to camouflage his wealth. Certainly the candy-pink woodwork ornamented with witch-balls and warming-pans was curious to say the least. It could also have been part of Van Meegeren's macabre sense of humour. A compulsive gambler in his earlier days, he had often bought lottery tickets, Now he purchased several of them regularly every week with much ostentation and boasted that he had won large prizes on a number of occasions. In this way he tried to explain his higher standard of living.

It has been said that Van Meegeren collaborated with the Germans in the war. There is absolutely no evidence of this. On the other hand, his daughter worked for the Dutch Resistance and was twice arrested by the Germans during the war, while her father certainly made a fool out of Goering. It was the picture he sold to Goering which in the end brought about his downfall. The Dutch authorities got to hear of this and suspected that, against their own decrees, works of art had been smuggled out of the country into enemy hands.

Painstakingly the Dutch police investigated the whole affair and this brought them on the track of Van Meegeren, for in their inquiries it was his name which popped up over and over again. It was noted that Van Meegeren had become an extremely wealthy man and that, for years, he had tried to hide this fact. He had bought one of the loveliest houses on Amsterdam's main canal and stocked it with beautiful antiques—genuine items this time. The Dutch authorities decided after the liberation of Holland that Van Meegeren must have collaborated with the enemy and that this was how he made his fortune.

He was arrested, but was swiftly able to disprove the charges of collaboration and he then made the confession that, far from having stolen the pictures by Vermeer, he had painted them.

This perhaps was Van Meegeren's greatest hour. Neither the police nor the art experts believed him. They were furious that they could not make the charges of collaboration with the enemy stick, but they felt sure they could trap him on stealing works by the great master and selling them abroad against the law.

All this time Van Meegeren had been held in prison. Highly strung, in indifferent health, accustomed to taking sleeping pills and alcohol, prison life told on him more than most. This undoubtedly was one reason why he made his confession. But beyond this he wanted above all to prove himself, to throw his critics into confusion and to saviour his triumph.

"Van Meegeren," they told him, "you are a liar. How can you say you have painted these pictures when they have been authenticated as genuine Vermeers by the highest in the land? Nobody has ever suggested you have that kind of talent."

"Nevertheless, it is true and I can prove it," he replied.

"Very well, then, will you actually copy a Vermeer in public?" inquired one critic, confident that this question would call his bluff.

"I will do better than that. I will paint another Vermeer."

Thus began one of the most curious artistic experiments of all time. Van Meegeren was let out of prison and allowed to return to his studio where, under surveillance, he was told to make good his boast. The authorities supplied him a seventeenth century canvas, The requisite oils and the proper brushes and the painter began his "new Vermeer" before witnesses representing the police, the civil authorities, the art museums and art critics. In two months, without having any models, he had completed another Vermeer entitled "Jesus Preaching in the Temple".

This did not settle the controversy in the minds of the authorities. The art critics were furious and insisted that Van Meegeren could not have got away with his forgeries to make the kind of high-figure sales he had obtained. The legal authorities then decided to appoint an international committee of inquiry. After X-raying and chemically analysing the disputed pictures the committee eventually revealed their findings at Van Meegeren's re-opened trial. Their reluctant verdict was that he had, without a shadow of doubt, painted the pictures which had been accepted as masterpieces. The painter had won his private war against the art critics and experts.

How had he got away with it for so long? Dr. H. J. Plenderleith, then Keeper of the British Museum Research Laboratory and a member of the investigating committee, expressed the opinion that Van Meegeren had succeeded in his hoax because of his brilliant scientific techniques for tackling the project, and especially his being able to reproduce the vivid colouring so reminiscent of Vermeer's work, together with the fact that, its being wartime, original Vermeers were not available for comparison.

If he had his moment of triumph, Van Meegeren still had to pay some kind of penalty. He was found guilty of faking fourteen Dutch masterpieces in all and selling them for a total of 7,167,000 guilden and sentenced to a year's imprisonment in October, 1947.

There was a wave of sympathy for Van Meegeren after sentence was passed. Many rejoiced that the art critics had been fooled. Others relished the thought that Van Meegeren had conned vast sums of money out of the Nazi leaders. Very many felt sorry for the man, now in his late fifties, whose health had obviously suffered while in prison. Suddenly, his own genuine paintings, which hitherto had been rejected or scorned by public and art critics alike, began to earn more money. Curiously enough, he had managed to sell some of his genuine pictures to the Nazis, possibly because he was able to read their minds so well that he knew exactly what type of paintings would appeal to them.

"I am convinced he was hounded to an early death," said his daughter. "It is ironic, for there were fabulous offers waiting for him in America. The Americans loved the joke. I still like to think of it as a joke, for if you don't laugh at a thing like that, you cry."

On December 30th, 1947, Van Meegeren died of a heart attack in an Amsterdam clinic. Since then, both his own works and his forgeries have become celebrated. In 1957 one of his paintings fetched £200 in an auction, not a huge sum, but one which Van Meegeren would have dearly liked to obtain when he was a young and struggling artist. In 1961 the British Museum opened an exhibition of forgeries, including a Vermeer by Van Meegeren.

13

THE SKULL WHICH CAUSED A SCANDAL

IF THERE is a lesson which con-tricksters down the centuries have to teach us it is, quite simply, not to trust experts. At least, not to put total faith in them. In wars it has often been the generals who have blundered, while the amateur politicians have been right. But in the sphere of science one is often up against the bigoted expert who blindly and stubbornly insists that he is right and tends to hide mounting evidence that he is wrong.

Indeed, scientific experts can be much more pig-headed, certainly more vain, and often less concerned about the truth than art experts. For if the latter were proved wrong in the case of Van Meegeren, how much more wrong—possibly even criminally wrong—were the scientists who for forty-one years accepted that the Piltdown Skull proved man's missing link with the apes.

It is true that those who subscribed to this theory based on a discovery in the Sussex countryside had had something to study before embarking on their fraud, yet this fact alone ought to have warned the scientists and experts that they should have been on their guard against deception. It seems merely to have led some of them to underwrite that deception, knowing that the evidence was false.

The first comparable case of this kind was that of the Onondaga Valley Giant of the 1860's, which for some years fooled a large number of people in the United States. A cigar-manufacturer named George Hull had then decided to create a specimen of the kind of giants described in the Old Testament. He ordered a stone-worker to carve out a naked giant from a huge block of gypsum. To make the giant's carcase seem genuinely ancient, sulphuric acid was used to stain the gypsum. Hull then had the artificial giant buried in the Onondaga Valley and left it for a whole year. Eventually it was dug up on October 15th, 1869, and Hull made a fortune charging people half a dollar a time to see the giant which he exhibited in a huge marquee.

While this hoax lasted Hull made quite a lot of money and he even managed to deceive two professors from Yale University who considered themselves to be authorities on fossils and palaeontology. Sooner or later, however, the inevitable happened: someone less gullible than the two professors demanded a sample from the giant so that he could analyse it. Having carried out his tests, he pronounced it to be gypsum.

It was a newspaper clipping about the hoax perpetrated by George Hull which many years later was found among the papers of a deceased Sussex solicitor. Certain passages of the clipping were underlined and it seems not too difficult to deduce from this that the solicitor in question had studied the case of the Onondaga Valley Giant with a view to seeing whether he could do better.

It was, of course, Charles Darwin who started off the hunt for man's link with the apes when he published his book, which created a great sensation at the time, called *On the Origin of Species*. His theory was, quite simply, that creatures evolve according to the conditions under which they live and that man himself had evolved from the apes. The idea, which seems relatively commonplace today, was sensational in the last century because it offended the principles and dogmas of those religious bigots who dominated society. To agree with Darwin was, in some circles, tantamount to blasphemy, a sin that exceeded those of the cities of the plain!

But it resulted in enthusiastic palaeontologists digging up prehistoric burial places in a quest for the missing link—an ancient skull that would prove to be half man and half ape. And in 1912 it seemed as though Darwin's thesis was not only vindicated, but that established proof had been made of man's missing link with the apes. It all happened in a gravel pit a little way off the main road between Chailey and Lewes in Sussex and there to mark the spot and confirm the legend for the best part of half a century a stone plaque stated:

"Here in the old river gravel Mr. Charles Dawson, F.S.A. found the fossil skull of Piltdown Man 1912-13."

It was not the only memorial to this discovery. An old inn which used to be known as The Lamb changed its name to that of Piltdown Man, flaunting a sign that depicted an unshaven brute in an orange skin throwing a rock at a beast with two horns. But perhaps the biggest tribute to Piltdown Man was the bibliography of more than 300 items devoted to the subject.

In the previous century, scientists had been hostile to the idea of a "missing link". Possibly they remembered the pupils of Johann Beringer of Wurzburg who decided to play tricks on their tutor by manufacturing fossils and burying them in the ground. Beringer was not only taken in, but he published a book in 1726, describing the fossils. When he realised he had been the victim of a practical joke, he spent much of his money buying up all the remaining copies of his book.

But by the early twentieth century scientific opinion had achieved a kind of consensus in accepting that somewhere the missing link could be found. So when Charles Dawson, a country solicitor and clerk to the local Magistrates' Court, dug up four pieces of cranium, a jaw, nine remnants of what appeared to be animal teeth, five flints and a canine tooth, scientists of the day took immediate notice. This was what they had been looking and hoping for.

Dawson had been an amateur palaentologist and geologist for several years. At the age of twenty-one he had been made a Fellow of the Geological Society and almost all his spare time had been spent digging up fossils and the like. His story was that one day he happened to mention to some workmen who were mending a road that he was a collector of fossils and that if they came across any, would they let him know. While working on a gravel pit one of the men came across what seemed to be part of a human skull. He gave it to Dawson.

That was in 1908. "Three years later," said Dawson, "I paid another visit to this site and I found another and larger piece of bone." This, together with various other subsequent finds, Dawson reported to Dr. Arthur Smith Woodward (later Sir Arthur), the famous palaeontologist. Later that summer of 1912 Dawson showed Woodward the site and together with a young French priest called Teilhard de Chardin they hunted for other relics of the dawn of man.

Suddenly it was accepted that these finds added up to the fact that the earliest man had the cranium of a human being and the jawbone of an ape. A large crowd assembled in the lecture room of the Geological Society in Burlington House on December 18th, 1912, to hear Woodward and Dawson proclaim the discovery of *Eoanthropus Dawsoni*—Dawson's dawn man. Woodward, as well as Dawson, told how animal remains had been found and made a reconstruction of what he thought early man would have looked like.

There were a few who disagreed with Woodward's assertations, but they were outnumbered by those who went along with him. One man who had slight doubts was Sir Arthur Keith, Conservator of the Hunterian Museum of the Royal College of Surgeons. He was somewhat upset that Woodward had been rather secretive about so important a find in the early stages. One complaint was that Woodward had only shown the objects to him for twenty minutes before he gave his Burlington House lecture. He made various criticisms after the lecture, one point being that if the canine were to be discovered, a more realistic assessment of the jaw would be possible.

Then, surprisingly, the actual canine was discovered immediately afterwards. Not by Dawson, or Woodward, but by Teilhard de Chardin, the French priest, later to become famous as the great Jesuit philosopher. He, too, was an enthusiastic amateur palaeontologist who had helped Dawson and on August 30th, 1913, he found a canine which proved more or less to match that of the model which Woodward had reconstructed.

Other finds followed over the next few years. One of the most surprising was an elephant bone which had been shaped into a prehistoric tool, claimed to be the earliest implement made of bone ever found. Then in 1915 Dawson turned up the tooth of a rhinoceros in a nearby field. A year later the solicitor died. His fame was commemorated in the British Museum by a glass case containing the skull of Piltdown Man and 300 copies of this skull were sent to museums all over the world.

Despite the discovery of the Java Man skull in 1936 and that of Peking Man in 1938, the reputation of Piltdown Man lasted until after two world wars. But in 1948 a geologist named Dr. Kenneth Oakley, who had been working in the British Museum, asked for permission to carry out some tests on the Piltdown skull. By this time Sir Arthur Smith Woodward had died, but his book about Piltdown Man, *The Earliest Englishman*, published in 1948, had raised certain doubts. Oakley submitted Piltdown Man to fluorine tests, carbon dating and nitrogen analysis. The verdict was devastating: the first shock was that the bone was only 50,000 years old, not half a million as had been previously accepted. When the tests had been completed Oakley, together with two friends, Dr. J. S. Weiner and Sir Wilfrid Le Gros Clark, were convinced that the Piltdown Man was a fake.

As a result, in November 1953, Clark, Oakley and Weiner issued a signed report in the Bulletin of the British Museum which bluntly stated: "Many experts believed the Piltdown Skull to be genuine. It is now clear that they were the victims of a most elaborate and carefully prepared hoax."

They went on to assert that the jaw came from a modern ape, probably an orang-utan, made to look old by being stained with chemicals. The upper part of the skull probably belonged to a stone age man; the tool said to have been made out of an elephant's bone had been cut with a metal knife, while the rhinoceros tooth possibly came from somewhere in Tunisia. All these and many other of the items discovered around the Piltdown site must have been placed there by a faker.

But who was the faker? Who was the con-trickster who had made fools of the experts for more than forty years? Or were there two or more hoaxers? The scientists who were so anxious to prove Piltdown Man a fake were surprisingly coy when it came to naming names. Perhaps scientists, like trade unionists, tend to stick together. The nearest anyone got to hinting at names was Weiner when he declared that "the joker must be one of the people we know to be connected with Piltdown Man." This suggested that it could have been Charles Dawson or Sir Arthur Woodward, both of whom were dead.

It was clear that the hoax could only have been perpetrated by someone who had studied geology and had considerable knowledge about fossils and the type of test carried out on such finds in the first decade of the twentieth century. This applied to either Dawson or Woodward. Whoever carried out the faking was not motivated by a desire to make money, but much more probably by a wish for fame. And immortal fame, though in the end it turned sour, becoming notoriety, was what both Dawson and Woodward obtained, the former with plaques and world-wide credit for the finds, the latter with a knighthood and international repute.

Dawson was the favourite candidate for the hoaxer in many people's minds. True, he had his defenders who pointed to his highly respectable reputation as a solicitor and a citizen, and they launched bitter attacks on anyone who dared to impugn him. But others began to remember curious incidents about Dawson. One recalled that in his solicitor's office "there was a queer 'kitchen' in a corner of his room. It was only a large saucepan and a gas-ring, but all day long strange, old bones simmered in it. When a client came to see him, he would turn off the gas and switch it on again when he left."

It was also recalled that Dawson was making finds of one kind and another all his life, with such frequency in fact that he had been nicknamed "the Sussex Wizard". How was it that he managed to discover so many remarkable things in the course of his spare-time digging? Apart from all the items that added up to Piltdown Man, there were countless flints, "Roman bricks", a petrified toad encapsulated in a flint, the tooth of a unique creature, half mammal and half reptile that he called *Plagiaulex Dawsoni* and countless other finds. Circumstantial evidence suggests that Dawson's chief scientific talent was deception and that he was a compulsive, but nonetheless brilliant and well organised hoaxer.

A little later, proof that he was a forger was provided in an unexpected manner, not by an examination of old bones, or fossils, but of a map. This was one published in the *Sussex Archaeological Collections* of 1912: it was described as "a copy of a map of the Maresfield Forge in 1724, made by C. Dawson, F.S.A." When carefully examined in 1974, exactly half a century later, Lieut.-Col. P. B. S. Andrews, a Sussex historian, was able to prove that Dawson's map was "clearly an outrageous fraud, not possibly copied from any genuine original map of 1724, and containing many anachronisms dating right down to the closing years of the nineteenth century as well as a vast deal of other fantastic rubbish".

So Dawson was at last convicted of forgery on one count by having fabricated a bogus early eighteenth century map.

Was this the beginning of Dawson's career of faking, or was it just one of many examples of his forgeries over the years, many of which are possibly still undetected? One suggestion is that Dawson did this to revenge himself on the Sussex Archaeological Society who had boycotted him and his antiquarian works, tricking them into publishing a fraudulent historical map. Lieut.-Col. Andrews also thought that an early discovery of a Roman statuette by Dawson, rejected as being a fake by the British Museum, was a traumatic blow to his self-esteem. Dawson was then a young man. He had bought the statuette in the belief that it was genuine. "I think that from the moment his statuette and antiquarian judgement were discredited Dawson resolved to become the master faker, able to fool the wisest expert in any subject with rubbish far less plausible than the statuette."

But even this revelation did not convince all the experts that Dawson was the faker of Piltdown Man. Some thought he could only have brought off his coup with the connivance of Sir Arthur Smith Woodward. This is a possibility, though it is more likely that Woodward subconsciously wanted to believe Dawson and subdued any doubts he may have had, as he just could not resist playing the role of part-discoverer of Piltdown Man.

Dr. Glyn Daniel, of St. John's College, Cambridge,

wrote to *The Times*, casting doubt on the view that Dawson was the Piltdown forger. He stated that his list of those who might be guilty, apart from Dawson, "includes Sir Arthur Smith Woodward, Professor W. J. Sollas, Horace de Vere Cole, Lewis Abbott, Father Teilhard de Chardin, Sir Grafton Elliot Smith, A. S. Kennard, W. H. Butterfield and Martin Hinton."

A formidable list of possible villains! In 1970 Professor James Leakey in his book *Unveiling Man's Origins* had suggested that there was more than one hoaxer and named Teilhard de Chardin as one of them. He pointed out that Teilhard was known to have been a practical joker and his friend, Father Pelletier had been a trained chemist and mineralologist. A member of Teilhard's family had also stated that there was a secret document compiled by Teilhard lodged in a bank in France which would be opened one day and might reveal a sensational story.

It is more than likely that the story of the secret document was Teilhard's kind of practical joking. The evidence strongly suggests that if anyone was taken in by the Piltdown discoveries it was Teilhard himself and that, if he discovered a fake, then someone else had planted it. In a letter to Dr. K. P. Oakley, Teilhard admitted that he had been deceived by his discovery, adding that "it spoilt one of my brightest and earliest palaeontological memories."

Nonetheless, religious controversy may have played a part in the Piltdown story. Sir Frank Colyer, who for fifty years was one of Britain's most famous dentists, said "I have always wondered if it [Piltdown] was connected with religious disputes over evolution".

In *The Harvard Crimson* of November 24th, 1953, Professor Hallam L. Movius stated that he did not believe for a single moment that Charles Dawson was the perpetrator of the hoax. "I'm only guessing," he added, "but I think the joker was one of the technicians in the

British Museum who had an ambition to fool the experts".

This widens the scope for positively identifying the forger, but it brings one no closer to finding a likelier candidate than Charles Dawson, with or without the collaboration of others. Even if others connived in his deception, Dawson must take the major credit for a quite remarkable imposture. Whatever theories others may propound, the truth is that no further Piltdown clues were found after Dawson's death in 1916. This alone points to Dawson. And if Dawson could fake an eighteenth century map and get away with it so easily in an archaeological magazine, read by experts, he obviously had the talent and aptitude of an astute forger. But there was even more damning evidence against Dawson unearthed by Dr. J. S. Weiner, when the latter was conducting his investigations. Weiner came across an old cabinet of flints that had belonged to a deceased bank clerk named Harry Morris, who was also an amateur archaeologist. One of the flints was identical to some of those found at Piltdown and on a tab was written: "Stained by C. Dawson with intent to defraud (all)—H.M." Another note stated: "Stained with permanganate of potash and exchanged by D. for my most valued specimen—H.M." Finally, there was this incriminating note: "I challenge the South Kensington Museum authorities to test the implements of the same patina as this stone which the impostor Dawson says were 'excavated from the pit'—H.M. Truth will out."

All this would seem to indicate that Dawson was the impostor who devoted several years to building up his discovery of Piltdown Man, but we may never be sure whether or not he had collaborators. Miss Mabel Kenward, another of the amateur archaeologists of the Dawson era, referred afterwards to "a dark-suited man who on many occasions could be found poling about in the Piltdown gravels". Was this mysterious stranger someone other than Dawson? Sir Arthur Woodward agreed that both he and Dawson were together "one warm evening in 1912 . . . when we both saw half of the human jaw fly out in front of the pick-shaped end of the hammer which he [Dawson] was using."

There is a brief footnote to this story tucked away in the list of suspects compiled by Dr. Glyn Daniel. It concerns the name of Horace de Vere Cole. It is highly improbable that he had the skill to be the Piltdown forger, though he certainly possessed the daring, impudence and imagination. For Horace de Vere Cole was *par excellence* the most imaginative practical joker of the twentieth century. He played so many jokes of this kind that it is not altogether surprising that he should be suspected as one of the Piltdown hoaxers.

Nothing at all has ever emerged to link his name with that affair, though it is not unlikely that he may have teased both his friends and his enemies by suggesting that he organised it. His biggest hoax was when in 1910 Cole, together with Duncan Grant, the artist, Anthony Buxton, Guy Ridley and Virginia Woolf, the author, fooled the top brass of the Royal Navy by posing as a party of Abyssinian princes on a visit to HMS *Dreadnought*. Cole arranged for Willy Clarkson's make-up men to prepare the disguises. At Weymouth the party was received by the C-in-C's Flag Lieutenant with cocked hat and sword, a guard of honour and a band. Once the party was back in London, Cole released the story to the press and telephone wires fairly hummed with angry inquiries when it was realised what had happened. Scotland Yard was alerted, the Admiralty was aghast and M.P.s. raised questions about security in the Navy.

Cole played many other pranks of a similar nature, but he hardly comes into the category of a con-trickster. He might very easily have become one of the world's greatest con-men, but he preferred raising laughs out of relatively harmless pranks to any serious conmanship.

14

MEN WHO COULD SELL YOU THE EARTH

THOUGH IN scientific and artistic circles confidence tricks are far more difficult to bring off today than they were a century ago, in some respects people are more gullible in the twentieth century than they were in the past. They seem to be particularly vulnerable to confidence tricks which take the form of salesmanship.

Perhaps sophisticated advertising has softened some of us up, or is there a psychological blind spot among a few people which makes them desperately anxious to buy the unobtainable? If someone told you that for twenty pounds cash down and no questions asked, you could have the deeds and title to a delectable uninhabited island in the Mediterranean, could you be sure you would not take a chance and buy it unseen?

The fact is that very many people have been conned into doing just this, especially in the Bahamas where some such miniature islands have no water and are infested with insects, and they have paid not a mere twenty pounds for something they haven't seen, but in some instances a few thousands. It might be said that all salesmanship is a kind of con trick, but it takes real genius and a master-mind of conmanship to sell bridges and public monuments which their owners, individual or municipal, have no intention of selling.

Yet there was a time when visitors to Istanbul would be asked to buy the Sophia Mosque, or some other notable landmark—and this was not so very many years ago either. But today Sulun Osman, formerly the most persuasive salesman in the city, has elected to "go straight". This remarkable man spent twenty-five years of his professional life in prison for his audacious "disposal" of famous buildings, monuments and public property to visitors to Istanbul.

It all reads rather like the type of outrageous fiction which any critic would savagely reject on the grounds that it described the impossible. For among the items that Sulun Osman sold were the famous Galata Bridge over the Golden Horn linking the two sides of Istanbul, two Byzantine fire-towers, the clocks in the city squares, the university building and the Simplon-Orient express.

In addition, he also sold such minor items as tram cars and the underground railway. His method of disposing of the clocks in the city squares, as he described it, was as follows:

"I waited under one of the clocks until someone stopped to correct his watch with the time shown. I asked him for 2.50 liras. He asked why and I told him that I owned the clock. While we were arguing, an accomplice, by an arrangement made earlier, came along, looked at the clock, set his watch by it and paid me 2.50 liras. The stranger then paid me also.

"He was a trader from Anatolia and, after further conversation, we went and had some coffee. He asked me how much I was making from the business. I told him I was making a fortune and in the end I sold him two clocks in Beyazit Square for the equivalent of a hundred pounds."

This was a terse and no doubt accurate description of the bare bones of Solun Osman's conmanship, but it omits (perhaps even through modesty) any detailed account of how he summed up the psychology of his victims. No doubt over cups of Turkish coffee he cleverly questioned them on what work they did, what their interests were and, more importantly, made probing inquiries which would reveal how their minds worked. For Solun Osman must have been a mind and character reader of such ability that, if he had wished, in could have outstripped all the astrologers and psychiatrists in existence. One wonders why nobody had not thought long ago of the rich harvest that could be reaped by employing a certain type of con trickster as a psychiatrist.

Solun attributed his success to his ability to judge quickly how naive a person is. "As long as there are people about with empty brains and full pockets, my kind will always succeed," he maintained.

In the early 1960's he was released from prison in a general amnesty and decided to concentrate on honest and orthodox enterprises. It is heart-warming to learn that the police, who worked for years to catch him, and newspapers who frequently enlivened their columns with stories of his exploits, collected money to buy him a shop. Then Solun settled down to a quiet, if dull life, while using his expertise and undoubted knowledge of the underworld to give occasional advice to the police on how to stop swindles.

An even more remarkable con-man was Arthur Fergusson, a Scot who started out in life as an actor. Probably he was one of those actors who have talent, but no real dedication and who soon found an easier way of earning money, a more profitable means of exploiting his own histrionic ability.

The story is that in the early 'twenties Fergusson, who had altered his name to that of Furguson, met an American from Iowa in Trafalgar Square. The latter was looking up at Nelson's Column and taking snapshots. Fergusson, who was out of work at the time, recollected that recently he had played the part of an

American who had been exploited by a conman. The idea flashed across his mind that here seemed to be a gullible character and that he might try some conning himself.

No doubt at first he just saw this as an actor's joke. He went up to the American and casually commented: 'Magnificent statue, isn't it?"

"Sure," replied the man from Iowa. "Who is the guy?"

"That is England's greatest hero, Admiral Lord Nelson, the man who won the Battle of Trafalgar and this square is named after it. That is the pride of all London. What a crying shame that very soon it will have to come down."

"But why?"

"These are hard times. England is suffering more than most from the depression and Nelson's Column has got to be sold. You see, we owe a vast war debt to the United States and we need to earn dollars to pay it off."

"But surely the people will cut up rough if their national monument is sold."

"They would, but they won't know anything about it until all has happened. It is being kept very hush-hush for that reason."

Then the American asked the very question that Fergusson hoped he would ask: "How do you know all this?"

Fergusson spun a story that he was "an official agent of the British Government" and responsible for the sale of Nelson's Column and other monuments in London. When the sale was announced officially there would be quite a rush of prospective buyers, especially from overseas. The American was immediately interested. Could he get in a bid in advance of the auction, sale or what have you? He would very much like to buy the statue and set it up in his home town in Iowa, with a plaque that named him as the donor. Fergusson said he would have to consult with top Civil Servants, but that if the man from Iowa would like to name a figure, he would let him know the answer the following day.

For six thousand pounds, written out by cheque and speedily cashed by Fergusson, Nelson's Column was, according to an official looking receipt, sold to the Iowan. Only when he set about arranging for the statue to be dismantled and transported across the Atlantic did the American learn what kind of a trick had been played upon him.

Arthur Fergusson, as he was always known afterwards, is alleged to have made one more attempt at the "big sell" while in London. This time another American called in the police and complained that he had paid one thousand pounds for Big Ben, but that no contractor would remove it for him, and one had suggested he ought to be locked up! From London Furguson went to New York, where he tried to sell the Statue of Liberty in New York Harbour to an Australian. But here Furguson overeached himself and ended up with a five year prison sentence.

The ace of all salesmen con-tricksters was undoubtedly Victor Lustig, more generally known as Count Lustig, a man with twenty-four aliases operating on both sides of the Atlantic. His greatest achievement was that he sold the Eiffel Tower. Not once, but twice!

He has been described as "the greatest con-man in the history of American crime". His victims ranged from bank presidents to Al Capone. He was elegant, charming, eloquent, adventurous, sophisticated, a man of the world who could speak five languages fluently. For many years it was his proud boast that he had been arrested on forty-seven occasions, but had not a single conviction to his discredit. Such was the record of the seemingly unbeatable Count Victor Lustig at the height of his career.

This cosmopolitan salesman was born in Bohemia in

1890, the son of the mayor of Hostinné. As a student he was far too indifferent to hard work to shine, but he had a remarkably effortless talent for learning languages. He was a good mixer, had a persuasive and agreeable manner and, having expressed a desire to travel, his father sent him to Paris.

The trip to Paris was ostensibly to study at the Sorbonne, but Victor Lustig was determined from the very beginning to enjoy life and to do so by exploiting the many credulous people in the world. "I have worked it out", he told a friend on one occasion, "that there are tens of thousands of people in this world who can be fooled all the time. Of these, many are wealthy. The problem is finding them. Once one has discovered the answer to that, the rest is easy: the good life, cigars and champagne lie beckoning. Now I have developed a talent for recognising these people. It isn't easy, it takes considerable practice and know-how. But each year, each month, each day it gets simpler to spot the type of person who can be persuaded into the rashest of schemes."

Certainly, Lustig lived up to this policy. At first he operated mainly at the card tables, especially aboard ships crossing the Atlantic. The luxury cruising ship was what he concentrated on and he developed a shrewd eye for spotting card players who could be persuaded into playing for stakes beyond their means. Lustig was an expert card player and invariably managed to win all the vital games when the stakes were highest.

Throughout World War I Lustig lived in Paris, where his life was somewhat of a mystery. It is thought that he did some spying for the French and the Americans. Afterwards he emigrated to the United States and became an American citizen. Here he often posed as the suave, polished, spatted, monocled and silver-caned Bohemian nobleman, Count Victor Lustig, cunningly depending on a streak of snobbism in the American character. Once again he kept an eye open for the gullible and credulous and succeeded in making quite a lot of money out of some dubious deals. More than once he was in serious trouble with the law, but he managed to talk himself out of the most difficult situations.

He was a meticulous operator who planned his confidence tricks with almost military precision. He enjoyed good wines and food, but never allowed himself to drink too much. One of his maxims was that to win friends and influence people one must never appear to be anything other than spellbound by other people's interests. "Everybody likes a good listener," he said. "It is sometimes thought that the great confidence trickster is the man who can talk the most. This just isn't true. The greatest confidence trickster is the man who can listen, the man who can allow the other chap to talk himself into being tricked."

Soon Europe once more beckoned the dapper Bohemian with his talent for spotting the suckers of this world. Back in Paris, staying at the Hotel Crillon after having made a killing on a gambling ploy in Canada, Lustig read with interest of the French Government's concern about the high costs of maintaining the Eiffel Tower. This news item set him thinking up a new project. It was outrageous, yet in essence quite simple: at least, that is how it seemed to Lustig. He would apply himself to exploiting the maintenance problems of the French Government to find someone who would be prepared to buy the Eiffel Tower. All that was required was a carefully worked out scenario by which he could lure prospective customers.

But the kind of customers Lustig had in mind on this occasion was not the gullible, the credulous or the eccentric, but the hard-headed businessman to whom the Eiffel Tower would mean nothing at all as long as he could pull it down and make a fortune by doing so. This was where Lustig was always so clever. He had an unerring gift of knowing exactly what kind of a person could be persuaded to buy such a national monument.

Not long afterwards, five scrap-iron dealers of ack-knowledged business acumen received letters on faked *Ministére des Postes et Telegraphes* letter-headings, requesting them to come to the conference room at the Hotel Crillon to be given details of a Government contract. When they arrived they found Lustig seated at a table with an assistant. After offering them refreshments and drinks, he announced that for security reasons no details of the contract had been given in the letter. However, the purpose of the conference was to give them all an opportunity to consider putting in tenders for the dismantling of the Eiffel Tower, which had become far too expensive to maintain, and to sell it as scrap iron.

"Gentlemen," said Lustig gravely, "as you will appreciate, this question of dismantling a celebrated national monument, famed all over the world, is a delicate matter. It is a painful decision which the Government has had to make and it requires considerable tact in handling affairs. The Government has entrusted me with the negotiations and you five gentlemen have been selected to hear the details not merely because you and your firms are capable of undertaking the project, but because you are known for your integrity and discretion."

The scrap-iron merchants were aghast at the news that the Eiffel Tower was to be scrapped, but they listened to the extraordinarily detailed account of the edifice, including weights and measurements and informantion on stresses and strains which Lustig rattled off at high speed. After that they were taken on a tour of the Eiffel Tower. This tour was planned partly to impress the dealers, but also to give Lustig a chance of getting to know each man better so that he could select his likeliest victim.

The bids were eventually delivered personally to

Lustig, as he had asked, the following day. Lustig did not accept the highest bid, but chose as his victim a dealer named Poisson who had given all the indications of being somewhat of a social climber, anxious to ingratiate himself in the highest circles of Ministries and Governments.

A deal was arranged and a splendidly impressive concocted document for the contract, drawn up on Government paper, was duly handed over. Poisson not only handed over a certified cheque for a considerable sum, for which he had mortgaged his property, but a cash commission for Lustig. As Poisson left the hotel, Lustig's luggage was loaded into a car outside the Crillon and soon the bogus Count was speeding away to Vienna, but not before the cheque had been cashed.

Lustig had chosen his man well. Poisson was too ashamed to make a fuss. Either he did not wish to reveal himself as a fool, or he wanted to conceal how much money he had lost. Thus Lustig got away with his masquerade without the story of his hoax ever getting into the newspapers, let alone being followed up by the police. Most men would have left well alone and been glad with this single success. Not Lustig. Sometime afterwards he returned to Paris and tried once more to sell the Eiffel Tower. But this time the police intervened and he had to return to the United States in a hurry.

Lustig did not always concentrate on the "big sell". His conmanship could sometimes descend to abyssmal depths such as getting dozens of petty thieves to act out a successful gaming den to fool some wealthy innocent. Some of his minor coups were simple individual operations, like knocking on hotel rooms and saying, "I'm the hotel detective, why aren't you two married? OK, give me a couple of grand and I'll say nothing."

But eventually even this precise operator became careless and over-confident. His second attempt to sell the Eiffel Tower should have been a warning to him.

But, having duped Al Capone, at that time America's No. 1 gangster, out of £1,500, he came to regard himself as a super-man of the criminal world. On his forty-eighth arrest he had his first conviction—a 20-year sentence at the dreaded Alcatraz Prison for issuing 1,340,000 counterfeit dollars. This ambitious project not only alarmed the powers that be at Fort Knox, but brought the Federal Bureau of Investigation on Lustig's trail in 1934.

Lustig spent eleven years in jail before he died. On his death certificate was a curious entry which might almost have been made as a sardonic joke by Lustig himself: he was described as an "apprentice salesman."

15

WHEN CHARITIES LOSE THEIR HALOES

IN NO sphere in modern times has the con-trickster been more active than that of charity. Moses ben Maimon (1135-1204) wrote: "Anticipate charity by preventing poverty, assist the reduced fellowman, either by a considerable gift, or a sum of money, or by teaching him a trade, or by putting him in the way of business so that he may earn an honest livelihood, and not be forced by the dreadful alternative of holding out his hand for charity. This is the highest step and the summit of charity's golden ladder."

Alas, even in this so-called enlightened twentieth century so sane a policy is not altogether adopted. Charity has been more the happy-hunting ground of the con-trickster in the second half of the twentieth century than ever it was before. Much of the trouble is due to two factors: firstly, it is too easy to start a charity fund and, secondly, most of the laws relating to charity in all countries have changed little in the past hundred years.

A situation has been reached in the United Kingdom today where, according to their terms of reference, the Charity Commissioners have to declare a good deal of charitable work as being outside the laws of charity. It is in Britain, perhaps more than anywhere else that advantage has been taken of the chaotic state of the charity laws, the duplication of work and downright corruption. In the U.S.A. there has been a move towards a kind of Community Chest structure which prevents the worst type of abuses. Yet in Britain, even fifteen years after the last Charities Act of 1960 was passed, when it was made compulsory for most charities to register, nobody knows how many local charities there are. Thousands of unsuspected societies have sprung up all over the country and hundreds of them have not even been registered.

There are today 114,000 registered charities in Britain alone. Up to 1973 it was estimated that forty-five new charities were being registered each week. Their annual income is about £150,000,000. An interesting aspect in the changing face of charity is that today the emphasis is often on helping what some would call the least deserving rather than the most deserving sections of society. This may seem an oversimplification, but drug addicts, ex-prisoners, juvenile delinquents, sexual misfits and even hardened criminals sometimes seem to rate more than the rest of the less fortunate members of society. This provides considerable scope for exploitation by the con-trickster.

It is extraordinarily easy to start a charity and, in the United Kingdom at least, the law again plays into the hands of rogues. Anyone can set up a charity, providing that its aims come under the official definition of a worth-while purpose. Generally, this means setting up a limited company, trust, society or incorporated association and then applying to the Charity Commission in London. The Commission has no powers to refuse registration, providing an organisation is established for public rather than private benefit. Once recognised as a charity, you are then exempt from income tax, corporation tax, capital gains tax and also qualify for some rates relief. It is another bonus for the conman that certain types of charity do not require to be registered. The Charity Law Reform Commission estimates that about 90,000 charities can avoid registration.

It takes all kinds to make a charity: sometimes the founders of charities are themselves eccentric, sometimes charities are founded on bizarre ideas. There are all manner of anomalies. The British Goat Society, Bromley Pleasant Sunday Afternoon and the Spiritual Regeneration Movement are legitimate charities; the Disabled Income Group, the Campaign Against Racial Discrimination (C.A.R.D.) are not. It is even possible for a group practising black magic to receive tax relief on covenanted donations, while more genuine societies cannot qualify for this. As for the really zany charities, it is astonishing how long these have managed to survive. Those in the City of London for killing lady-birds on Cornhill and for the burning of heretics were cleared away nearly a hundred years ago, but in a Derbyshire village green and grey waistcoats are still given to the needy from funds bequeathed by Thomas Green and Thomas Gray. In Kent there is a charity for providing red flannel petticoats for the virgins of the parish. Time has played tricks with some of the bequests of long-forgotten philanthropists. There is the case of the Maid's Money of Guildford. In 1674 John How decided that two serving maids should throw a dice and the winner should benefit from his charity. But in 1702 John Parsons set up a fund for the loser. John Parsons' charity flourished and the loser now gets more than the winner!

Societies which qualify as charities include one which supports the doctrines of Swedenborg, another which promotes the art of embalming, the search for the hypothetical Bacon—Shakespeare documents and even the society that maintains the beliefs of Joanna Southcott and her celebrated box of secrets. In such a variform and even exotic environment it is not surprising that the con-trickster has come into his own.

One of the spheres of charity into which the con-trickster has penetrated deeply is that which concerns racialism, aid to underdeveloped countries and assistance to the downtrodden. Great objection has been taken in recent years to the definition of charity in Britain under Queen Elizabeth I, which laid down that it should cover "activities beneficial to the community of the United Kingdom". This has led to clashes between the Charity Commissioners and the Joint Standing Conference of British Organisations for Aid to Refugees, and some tough legal battles have ensued. The argument of the Commissioners has been :"It is all right for a British charity to help, say, a particular group of poor farmers in an overseas country by giving them tractors, buying corn or teaching them how to read and write, but it is not charitable to raise the general economic level by building roads, or irrigation schemes. This is dabbling in politics by doing the work of other governments at the expense of the British tax payer".

Various charitable organisations in Britain and elsewhere have been accused of sending goods and food overseas only to see them end up in the hands of racketeers and food hoarders and rarely reaching the starving millions for whom they were intended. "Shelter" has been attacked because it is linked with the politics of the housing shortage. It raises a million pounds a year. Does some of this money assist undesirable squatters through the exploitation of an ideal by quite unscrupulous conmen posing as friends of the underdog? It would appear that almost anything can happen in the world of charity so that an official of a society who is himself the soul of integrity may not know what is going on beneath the surface. A schoolteacher told a jury at Manchester Crown Court in September, 1972, that he could not remember being elected treasurer of a charity which was said to have collected almost £11,000 and paid out only

£726 in eighteen months. Two men were charged with conspiring to defraud and conspiracy to submit false and misleading returns about the charity.

Then there was the case of Robert Jones who had "visions" that Indian children in Britain were desperately in need of help. Believing that this guidance was a form of extra-sensory perception, he set up a fund to raise the money for a children's home. The Charity Commissioners accepted the registration of "Sanctuary" in the London borough of Ealing as a charity because it was not within their terms of reference to inquire into the reasons why. In June, 1971, the Commissioners had to inform Mr. Jones that he would be relieved of his office as a trustee of the fund. This was done not because of any doubt as to Mr. Jones' ability actually to find Indian child brides by clairvoyant means, as he claimed, but because expenses took up nearly all of the charity's income. Their inquiry had revealed "gross mismanagement" in the administration of the charity and that out of £5,759 collected by Sanctuary between July, 1968, and December, 1970, the sum of £5,155 had been swallowed up in expenses.

The Commission's watch-dogs operate in London and Liverpool, mainly to investigate charities they are not happy about. Where the investigators suspect fraud, they hand the matter over to the police. When they act themselves in freezing assets and appointing new trustees, as in the case of "Sanctuary", it is because they have found incompetence in management rather than criminal intentions. Trustees actually have to mismanage charities to be removed. A Sunday newspaper revealed in 1971 that a man with convictions for sexual assault had set up a charity to provide hostels for teenage girls. But there was nothing that could be done to stop him.

One of the worst cases of conmanship in the field of charity was that of the "Sympathy Salesmen" who claimed they helped pensioners, the blind and disabled, though their real aim was to help themselves. They took advantage of loopholes in the law to indulge in door-to-door salesmanship.

In 1972 the London *Daily Mail* claimed that more than ten million pounds a year was being milked from the public by doorstep salesmen who claimed to be offering goods made or packed by disabled people. The fact is that the Welfare State (to be found in its most bountiful and easily exploitable form in the United Kingdom), as it extends its boundaries across the world today creates a society that not only always has cash to spare for charity, but an increasing number of people to exploit this mass affluence. It would be interesting to know how many millions of the money donated to charities in the 1970's have gone into the pockets of con-tricksters.

This is perhaps the realm of the lowest grade of confidence trickster, with few redeeming qualities, so much so that one hesitates to include these crude and cruel operators among those artists in conmanship whose skill, and often their lack of greed, make redeeming characteristics. Yet it is important that they should be revealed, if only as an awful warning of how they are besmirching the very name of charity so that, sooner or later, there will have to be drastic laws to control all charitable activities.

Some of the worst swindles in the name of charity have been those associated with fund-raising for the relief of cancer. In 1974 two men and two women were jailed for a bogus cancer research charity, named the Imperial Cancer Fund, which netted them at least £3,000 in six weeks. This was largely raised by people going round public houses with collecting boxes. Donations varying between one pound and one half penny had been obtained from no fewer than 25,000 people.

The collecting box is one of the principal weapons of the charity confidence trickster who often pays good wages to his collectors, while taking a large slice of commission himself. In many cases it is almost impossible to prove that he is doing anything illegal. Often he can explain away his commission by saying that this is merely to recoup expenses in running the charity. Nor is it always confidence tricksters who claim excessive expenses in running charities. The Charity Commissioners have been unhappy about many highly respectable charities on the grounds that their administrative costs seem too high. But usually this means just a warning. In 1971, for example, their attention was drawn to the fact that expenses had taken £35,000 of the £72,000 raised towards a D-Day Memorial at Portsmouth Cathedral.

One of the cheekiest exploits was that of David King who decided to raise money for charity from his prison cell. He set a target of £30,000 to buy a seaside home for handicapped children. But King was already serving a year's jail sentence for fund-raising without a permit, and his plans were foiled by the Charity Commissioners. They refused to register his charity, named Greensleeves Trust.

When King was released from prison in March, 1975, he said "Perhaps I was being a bit too cheeky using the prison as my working base. Now all my efforts have been thwarted. But I had no difficulty in getting my Trust off the ground".

Not until new legislation is introduced will the world of charity be safe from its exploiters. Often the latter will emerge as professional organisers of fund-raising events such as gala performances, balls, sporting events and garden parties. The police themselves say that often they cannot touch these people even though they know they are probably making five thousand pounds for themselves for every five hundred pounds that goes to charity. A firm which was at one time collecting four hundred pounds a week for a kidney research charity paid out less than a thousand pounds over a period of two years, it was stated when at a creditors' meeting the firm, Charity Promotions (Kidney Research)Ltd., was said to have assets of £171 and debts of £8,006.

Sometimes charity organisers deliberately shelter behind some highly distinguished and well known name which they feel will give them an aura of genuineness. The Classical Literary Guild of Amsterdam, an organisation for which its English outpost claimed to have collected ten thousand pounds in less than fourteen weeks in Britain by linking the sale of magazine subscriptions to a children's charity, was one example of this. Established as a charity named the International Child Care Foundation, of which the Princess zu Hohenlohe became the patron, this organisation's real aim was to make money quickly.

At the heart of this magazine empire was Pierre André de la Faire, a tall, dark and handsome man who operated from a basement room in Amsterdam. He came from Indiana and planned to expand his fake charity drive into Britain and elsewhere. He also had plans to set up a headquarters in a hotel at Whitley Bay, Northumberland. Meanwhile at a meeting in Amsterdam, it was announced that the Foundation would assist children of all religions and nationalities in emergencies and make donations for crippled and mentally retarded children. La Faire pledged twenty per cent. of the profits of the Classical Literary Guild to the charity, guaranteeing payment of 1,500 guilders per month. But the Princess zu Hohenlohe, who had innocently agreed to become president of the Foundation, eventually had doubts as to La Faire's real motives. In 1969 she announced that La Faire "no longer had anything to do with the Foundation".

Eventually the hopes of the Classical Literary Guild were dashed by adverse press publicity and police investigation. Prosecutions followed swiftly and La

Faire's sales staff were swiftly disbanded when a number of the sales girls were charged with obtaining cheques dishonestly. La Faire himself hastily left Holland for Germany.

The assassination of Sheikh Mujibur Rahman, President of Bangladesh, was partly due to the gradual realisation of widespread corruption through the manipulation of charitable funds and goods by skilled conmen. While the Western world was proclaiming its belief in "gallant little Bangladesh" the less reputable supporters of the Sheik were exploiting this popularity to the fullest extent. One of Mujib's closest supporters was Gazi Ghulam Mustafa who proceeded as chairman of the Bangladesh Red Cross Society, to use the aid to ease distress in his country for his personal enrichment.

Gazi Ghulam Mustafa fooled all the do-gooders of the Western World with his chicanery. As chairman of the Ration Shop Distribution Committee, he allowed himself to be influenced by shopkeepers anxious to sell their foodstuffs on the black market. But this wily character extended his conmanship under various "hats"—those of chairman of the Dacca Improvement Allotment Committee, a member of the Abandoned Property Board and secretary of the Dacca City Awami League. As Mujib's friend, he was in a position to by-pass the law and to distribute homes and lands to those prepared to slip him backhanders for doing so.

All these stories are singularly unpleasant and it would seem to be an indisputable fact that the conmen who operate in the sphere of charity have few redeeming features.

16

THE FORGER WHO NEARLY RUINED A GOVERNMENT

IN THE early years of the emergence of a communist government in Russia a new school of conmen surfaced, comprising cosmopolitan adventurers and those skilled in the forging of false passports and documents. The Bolsheviks themselves indulged in this game, but it was anti-Bolshevik governments who were most exploited by this type of political conmen. Such was the hatred of communism that some politicians were prepared to believe anyone who spread sufficiently virulent reports of what the new Soviet Government was doing.

In one instance one of these conmen nearly brought about the downfall of a British Government. He was Thomas Walker, who arrived in London in the spring of 1934, claiming to be an American journalist who had been investigating life in Soviet Russia. He introduced himself to the American Trade Commissioner in London, who eventually gave him letters of introduction to various prominent people. Ostensibly, Walker's purpose was to sell articles and pictures based on his travels in Russia to show how grim life was in the Soviet Union. Such was the hostility of most newspapers and magazines to the communist regime in Russia at that time that Walker had little difficulty in arousing the interest of editors in his articles. In particular, he had convincing material and photographs showing conditions in the famine-hit Ukraine.

Walker made his headquarters at the American Club in Piccadilly, using their writing-paper on which to send out his letters. He was suave, well dressed, convincing and appeared to be a likeable and extremely well informed person. Apart from this, his passport revealed that he had been to Russia on a number of occasions.

Making friends with the wife of an influential British politician, Walker hinted to her that he had in his possession letters which showed that the then Prime Minister of Britain, Ramsay MacDonald, had, some years earlier, had "treasonable communications with the Russian Government".

Ramsay MacDonald had been leader of the British Labour Party and had formed the first two Labour administrations in Britain. During World War I he had been a pacifist and in his earlier years, it was true, he had shown sympathy to the aspirations of revolutionary Russia. Yet, by and large, Ramsay MacDonald was a moderate; indeed, his opponents inside his own party regarded him as far too conservative ever to introduce full-blooded socialism. When the world financial crisis hit Britain in 1931 MacDonald had put country before party and united with Tories, Liberals and some Labourites in setting up a National Government with himself at its head.

In 1934 MacDonald was still at the head of this coalition government, having won a resounding victory in a general election. Though in ill health and heading towards the end of his career, he was nevertheless an important figurehead whose very name maintained the legend of a genuinely "national" government. Thomas Walker could not have chosen a more devastating time for dropping this hint of political scandal, for another general election was drawing near.

The lady to whom Walker spoke suggested he should get in touch with Lady Houston, an extremely wealthy widow whose life was largely devoted to attacking socialism and communism. Anything in the nature of the letters of which Walker spoke could be guaranteed to make her take notice. She jumped at the bait with alacrity and paid Walker £5,000 for the letters with the intention of publishing them.

The first letter was typed on Ramsay MacDonald's private writing-paper from his home at Upper Frognal Lodge in North London. It was addressed to Grigori Sokolnikoff, who became the first Russian Soviet Ambassador to Britain at the Arcos offices in Moorgate, London, which were later raided by the police. This letter was as follows:

Dear Mr. Sokolnikoff, 11 February, 1926.

The time does not seem ripe for the movement you suggest. Everything is to be gained by a few months' delay. You may count upon me to support you in your noble work.

Sincerely,

J. Ramsay MacDonald.

This was a relatively innocuous letter, though it was one likely to arouse curiosity in the politically-minded. But the other letters were quite sensational and could have created not only a major political scandal, but possibly the downfall of the National Government. One letter, which sounded suspiciously like connivance in Soviet sedition in Britain, stated: "You must recognise that your Russian methods for serfdom and communism are not available for use here. Our British workman is more susceptable [sic] to worldly goods and materialistic enticements. It is my wish that this country may follow in the same course that you have chosen, but we must have a more intelligent introduction."

It was the third letter, dated March 5th, 1926, the

year of Britain's General Strike, that contained the real political dynamite. This was addressed to Christian Rakovsky, who had been Soviet diplomatic agent in Britain between 1923 and 1925 and was at that time Ambassador to France. This letter by MacDonald was written on House of Commons writing-paper and read: "Any change which is to readjust the allocation of wealth in Great Britain and which is to establish a system of justice in settling the relation between services and reward must be a sudden and violent change. I hope to see the day, not too far distant, when the King may follow the way of the Czar, but I do not feel too optimistic about the results of the general action planned for May."

Luckily, someone who examined these letters strongly suspected they were forgeries because, although a political opponent of MacDonald all his life, he knew that the Prime Minister had always had a high regard for the monarchy and a deep personal affection for King George V. That part of the letters which hinted at MacDonald wanting to see the King go the same way as the Czar—to assassination as well as abdication—did not ring true.

Unquestionably the letters were brilliant forgeries and handwriting experts testified to the skill with which MacDonald's signature had been forged. Scotland Yard was immediately called in and a thorough inquiry was carried out at high speed. The first step was to recover the letters from Lady Houston. This was not an easy matter, for that formidable lady was not to be deterred from her self-imposed anti-socialist crusade. When told that the letters were forgeries by a 'Yard inspector, she indicated that she was satisfied that the letters were genuine and she intended to publish them in her own periodical.

Meanwhile, other police officers had been making inquiries into Walker's background. It was learned that, though he had certainly been to Russia on a number of occasions, he had a false passport and had escaped from prison in Sing Sing in the U.S.A. It was also found that Walker's bills at the American Club were all unpaid. Armed with this information, Scotland Yard struck. They did not want a highly publicised scandal so they merely arrested Walker at his hotel in Knightsbridge as an undesirable alien with a false passport. He denied that the letters were forgeries and refused to say how they had come into his possession. He was given a month's imprisonment for travelling on a false passport and then deported. In New York the American police were waiting for him.

A skilful police operation prevented the story of the forged letters leaking out in open court. Nothing of this political scandal ever got into the newspapers. Eventually, Lady Houston was persuaded not to publish the letters and to give them to a firm of solicitors acting for the Prime Minister.

Walker had undoubtedly set about his massive con trick with determination and intelligence. In his hotel room were found notes as to how he should proceed with his plan and a list of names of people known to be hostile to the Prime Minister. As a forger he was in a class by himself and Scotland Yard never did find out just how he secured specimens of the Prime Minister's writing paper.

The confidence trickster who lived the longest must undoubtedly be Joseph Weill, who died peacefully in a nursing home in Chicago at the age of 100 in February, 1976. Nicknamed "Yellow Kid" Weill, this dapper and spruce operator earned his soubriquet because he was in the habit of wearing canary yellow gloves, yellow suits and ties when he took rooms at expensive hotels in all parts of America. He used such improbable aliases as "Sir John Ruskin Wellington", "Count Ivan Ivarnoff" and once had the cheek to take a name straight out of Robert Louis Stevenson when he called himself "Prince

Florizel of Bohemia".

In many respects Weill must go down as one of the brashest confidence tricksters of all time. It is true that he was often caught, but he never seems to have given up. Whereas there may have been many con-tricksters more successful in evading the law, more brilliant in their techniques, few can have shown such pertinacity, zeal and downright impudence. He carried on his tricks for at least half a century and some estimate that he totted up a sum of four million pounds all told in his lifetime. It is true that he spent most of his money, but he had enough left to end his last years in dignity and comfort. He not only inspired a number of writers by his exploits, but the film *The Sting*, in which Robert Redford and Paul Newman starred, was based on part of his life.

Perhaps the chief clue to Weill's success as a con-trickster is contained in his own philosophy which, he said, was based on the maxim "You can never cheat an honest man".

"A truly honest man would never have fallen for any of my schemes," he declared once. "I never fleeced anyone who could not afford my price for a lesson in honesty."

It certainly seems true that he never exploited the honest or decent people of the world, but always carefully chose his victims from among the greedy, the cunning and small-time crooks.

On one occasion he bought an abandoned quarry for a nominal figure and then fired gold dust pellets from a shot-gun into the recesses of the quarry. Having spread the word that the land contained gold and that he intended to develop a mine there, he sold shares in it to several gullible and greedy prospectors. Another time he tried out the same tactics on a stretch of the Chicago River and sold mining rights to fortune hunters.

Weill rented an abandoned bank, hired billiards hall customers as tellers and filled money bags with lead discs. Then, convincing a soap manufacture that he had established a bank, he conned him into putting a large sum of money on deposit at a high rate of interest. Sometimes such enterprises lasted only for a day, or a week at most, but one of his bogus brokerage offices actually traded for nearly twenty years.

Not surprisingly, such exploits resulted in his being caught on numerous occasions. Altogether Weill went to prison forty-one times, though he only served a period of six years in all. His last sentence was for 26 months in Atlanta for selling an oil well that only gushed water. When he came out of prison for that crime in 1941 he decided it was time to retire.

He had some scathing comments to make on big businessmen and bankers: "They are the biggest suckers in the world, because they are always looking for an easy way of making a quick dollar. Of all the people who can be conned, they are probably the easiest."

An exaggeration, no doubt, yet it would certainly seem to apply in the case of some big businessmen and some fringe bankers.

The advent of the Welfare State in Europe since World War II has paved the way to a new and fruitful ground for the con-trickster as well as the purely idle person. In Britain in particular, where the Welfare State often provides a better living for the unemployed person who knows his law than some hard-working, highly taxed artisans, the con-trickster has been much in evidence. But for the most part there has not been much artistry or skill in his exploits, nothing much to raise him above the level of the petty crook.

Surprisingly, the most brilliant coup against the Welfare State was brought off not in England but in France. For sheer audacity the record of Antonio Jimenez Moreno takes some beating. By forging birth certificates and school registration forms, he invented

197 fictitious families and more than 3,000 children on which he claimed benefits from 1960-68. Altogether he swindled the French Social Security system out of something like £2,300,000.

France wanted to put Moreno, or "El Chorro" (The Fountain) as he was nicknamed, in jail, but Moreno is living happily in Spain, which refuses to extradite him because he is a Spanish gypsy. "El Chorro" started life in a modest way, roving across France from Spain at the head of a gypsy tribe that stopped their caravans wherever there was work—harvesting, repairing cars or tractors and mending furniture. They never stayed anywhere long, as many French communes apply local laws which require nomads to leave town within forty-eight hours.

Like most gypsies, "El Chorro's" tribe had many children. Having children is profitable in France. The French family allocation, paid in cash once a month, is progressive, and intended to encourage large families. A father draws about seven pounds a month each for the first two children, rather more for the third and still more for the fourth. After that the sum per child stops growing, but it is paid for each child in the family, no matter how many. A family with modest tastes and a dozen children can live on the allocation alone, with no other source of income, and some families do just this. French nationality is not a requirement so long as the family lives in France.

Generous-minded French social workers have made things easier for gypsies than for families who are not so mobile. Having no fixed residence, the gypsies can register their children anywhere, when the child is born, or whenever they get around to doing it. In the early 1960's there was an influx of gypsies into France along with other refugees, when the French empire in North Africa ended. Many of these families were illiterate and some took years to find out about their rights under the

Social Security and family allocation laws and the need for registering for such benefits.

It was in this kind of situation that Antonio Moreno created his first opportunity to test out the Social Welfare system of France. His first venture into illegality was when he acquired the identity card of one Vicente Cortez, father of six children. Presenting himself as Cortez, Antonio applied for the six allocations. When a social worker—in a town where the gypsy tribe was merely staying overnight—came round to check up on the family, "El Chorro" displayed a few of his own children and a few of another gypsy, all of whom happened to be the right ages, and for which the tribe had long been collecting the allocations under their real names. The simple little confidence trick worked like a charm and Moreno began hunting for more identity cards.

Soon he acquired a large package of blank cards stolen from a Social Security office and from then on he manufactured children at will.

Ultimately, Moreno and half a dozen men who were his immediate subordinates in the tribe registered some 3,000 imaginary children. At least another 500 were registered by other gypsies who heard about the racket and copied Moreno's methods. There were accessory pay-offs, too. "Mothers" of the fictitious children collected pregnancy and maternity compensation. This was done by having one pregnant gypsy woman register in a dozen different towns, each time under a different name.

The vital statistics of this huge imaginary family were kept by Moreno in a single big ledger. He was meticulous, if nothing else. He recorded marriages, births and even deaths, apparently carried away by feeling the need for some kind of artistic verisimilitude in his gigantic work of fiction. All details were carefully written down so that no embarrassing mistakes could be made.

By 1968 this creative enterprise, sometimes embellished by delightful touches of imaginative real life details by

Moreno, was taking in something like £230,000 a year. The tribe was living high, but their bonanza was blown up when two of the men clashed in a knife fight and one was killed. Police moved in to investigate the killing and were amazed at the evidence of quite surprising wealth in the gypsy encampment. Probing for the source of these riches, they found "El Chorro's" ledger, from which they deciphered the names of 197 non-existent families for whose children the tribe was collecting allocations.

But "El Chorro" had been quick enough to anticipate that the police inquiry would eventually reveal his secret. When they came to question him, he had already disappeared. Indeed, it would seem that he had long ago believed that the most massive con-trick of modern times could not possibly last for ever. He had a great respect for French bureaucracy and he felt certain it would catch up with him in the end. So he had long since had the foresight to hide away much of his wealth in places known only to himself, presumably in Spain, where he turned up some time later.

Not all the gypsies were so lucky as this master-mind. Twelve of them were arrested and tried in France for taking part in the swindle. The French police requested the Spanish police to arrest Moreno. This they did, sending him to jail for three months for possessing a revolver. But a demand for extradition was refused on the grounds that a country does not extradite its own nationals. So today Moreno is a free man and a wealthy one. He owns and lives in a magnificent villa near Barcelona, wears diamond jewllery and a weighty gold chain.

But from the Moreno affair the French learned a lesson. They overhauled their family allocations system. Today ever gypsy family has had to apply all over again for any benefits, just in case there has been an attempt at a swindle. Every application is now sternly scrutinised.

17

AGE OF THE SCIENTIFIC CON-MAN

ONE OF the more alarming aspects of this latter half of the twentieth century is the manner in which science and the sophisticated world of the computer and the radar button, the thermal detector and the "harmonica bug" (a tiny transistorised eavesdropper which can be placed inside an ordinary telephone) have opened up new avenues for the con-trickster.

All this is not merely disturbing on a purely domestic level, but in the scope it provides for the conman to invade the realms of espionage, and especially commercial espionage, as well as threatening national security. In this age of *détente* and nuclear stalemate there must always be the lurking suspicion that the only way in which we could all find ourselves involved in a devastating, global nuclear war would be by somebody conning his way into a scrambled telephone, or by infiltration of a computer system.

If this seems far-fetched, one has only to consider some of the feats achieved by the modern, technologically educated con-trickster and the wide range of inventions which has put so many new devices before him. Bugging devices today are nearly all so tiny that they can be hidden in carpet tacks, wall lamps, cigarette packets and inside a bra. Bugging devices are relatively cheap and easy to handle; on the other hand, the gear for de-bugging is rather more formidable and costs far more. It has been through private industry and enterprise that bugging has been developed in recent years rather than by the Secret Services of the world. The latter have had to take steps to keep up with the commercial firms and this has entailed a high degree of commercial espionage carried out by the Intelligence Services.

Computers are so careless with money on occasions that in July, 1974, one was found to have mistakenly handed out more than three million pounds of welfare payments. It is probably true to say that computer crime was born with the machines: they pointed the way for tricksters to exploit them, for often the machines themselves were criminals.

The computer criminal is still evolving, to such a remarkable extent, in fact, that soon society will need a security organisation to protect people from being ruined by computers, whether this is through the "rogue elephant" element among the machines themselves which causes those astronomical telephone, electricity and gas bills, or the con-trickster who knows exactly how to "rig" or cheat the machines for his own ends. Not surprisingly the "white collar conman" was first to be found in banks where the computer still plays surprising tricks and sometimes tantalisingly refuses to stop a direct debit payment, however many times it may be ordered to do so.

One simple technique was to open bank accounts, obtain paying-in slips magnetically coded with their account numbers and then to leave these around among the blank paying-in slips on the bank's counters. If other customers used them to pay in and failed to realise that the account number was different from their own, the money would go into the swindlers' accounts. Astonishingly, this ruse worked for quite a time and one man got

£40,000 in this way. It could almost be argued that this was more an exploitation of other people's carelessness rather than a crime. Since then there have been added precautions to check this kind of thing.

Another man used a computer model of his firm to work out how he could best embezzle money without being detected, and then filled the books by hand according to the computer's instructions. For this con trick the accountant got ten years' imprisonment. Perhaps the most ingenious misuse of a computer listed in the SRI (Stanford Research Institute) of California study was the work of a New Hampshire University student who managed a delayed *coup d'état* within a computer. He incorporated a new unauthorised programme that lay dormant for six months until it was triggered off by an innocent user. It then destroyed all traces of how the programme had been placed there. This points the way to the most devastating exploitation of computers, especially in those countries where electronic know-how is of a far lower grade than, for example, in the United States.

Two men were jailed at the Old Bailey in February, 1971, for programming an accounts computer with fake invoices. What the computer had done was to pay out demands from Fountain Stores of Tooting for vast quantities of scampi, lobster and salmon which never existed. How long this particular fraud might have lasted, it is impossible to say. It was only discovered almost accidentally when a clerk took a look at the faked account number—00260—and sensed something unusual. By that time it was found that a catering firm had been defrauded by about £50,000.

At that time—such was the ignorance of people in Britain—it was actually claimed that this was the first case of a computer being used as an accomplice in fraud. But computer frauds had been snowballing all over the world for a long time prior to this. It is now suspected that many of the astonishing rises from poverty to riches in recent years—especially where these occur in areas of high taxation, such as the United Kingdom—have been manipulated through computer conning. Indeed, the excessive taxation has bred the crime. More and more individuals and firms are having to turn to specialists who can rescue or protect them from computer crimes. In the early 'seventies the turnover of Bellard Ltd., the computer security specialists, increased phenomenally, business going up by 800 per cent.

The fact was that in the 'sixties, when most of the get-rich-quick operations came to fruition, banks, business firms and even accountants took the view that the computer was an absolute guarantee against fraud. Once again the experts were wrong: they paved the way in for the criminals and nobody did more to lure people and Government departments into a false sense of security than the Institute of Chartered Accountants who blandly assured all that accountancy by computer would make for far greater accuracy and be a protection against fraud.

But computers do not possess morals: they do not discriminate between good and bad users. They may provide safeguards in some sections of accountancy, but they also unwittingly lay themselves wide open to exploitation by the unscrupulous in other areas. The fact is that the computer provided a far subtler and more effective method than the old time method of setting fire to accounts when in danger of being discovered; all the skilled con-trickster had to do with the computer was to run a magnet over the tapes, or to run them backwards. Another factor by which computer manipulation was made easier was that the frauds could only be detected by data processing managers and that accountants, having no knowledge of computerology, would not know where to start looking for errors or frauds. And in the early days of computer development in some countries experts were so scarce that, when one was recruited, any firm was glad enough to obtain his services, let alone to worry about his character, past record or a security clearance.

Yet as firms, banks and individuals began to catch up on the need to protect their computer systems from fraudulent exploitation, so do the con-men improve their tactics. There is no end to this war between the two sides and it is most in evidence in the relentless guerrilla warfare of computer-snoopers bent on securing commercial intelligence and lists of potential customers from rival firms. In the case of the two men jailed at the Old Bailey trial, they had almost certainly erred by inventing a new invoice number and it was this which had suddenly struck the inquisitive clerk as being odd. As this case became a classic of its kind it was carefully read by all computer con-men who immediately decided never to repeat this error. Since then more sophisticated perpetrators of computer frauds take the trouble to select an invoice number that has already been registered, though first carefully ascertaining that it is no longer in use. All they do is to alter the name and address of the supplier, client or what-have-you.

One American computer programmer, working for a bank, raised his overdraft limit by a mere three digits to 300,000 dollars. He only drew 180,000 dollars because he did not want interest to accrue so fast that the charges would place his account beyond the 300,000 limit, which it would if he had drawn too much. That would have attracted attention to his account. This programmer had calculated the risks carefully and worked out that his fraud could only be detected if a special request was made to the computer for it to print out a small block of names and, even then, only if his name happened to be on that particular list and somebody actually recognised it and identified him. The odds were tremendously against all this happening at one and the same time and for someone to be sufficiently interested to take notice.

Unfortunately for the programmer, this is what actually happened. In the ordinary course of events, rigid security rules applying to computers were such that an employee would be commiting an offence to examine the list of names on a print-out. An operator broke the rules and was furious to discover that a colleague had obtained such a high credit rating. Once he had gossiped to others about this, the fraud was soon discovered.

But, as will be seen, a system that depends on unique coincidences for fraud to be detected is extremely vulnerable. Probably it is surprising that there have not been more con-tricksters in this field where the pickings are potentially so rich. On the other hand, there is the possibility that there are far more such unscrupulous operators than is generally suspected and that many of them have not yet been caught. The awful truth is that when the con-trickster is the computer itself—a far too frequent happening in the world of inhuman machines—it is often exceedingly difficult to prove it is in the wrong. Anyone who has had an astronomically large telephone bill which makes sheer nonsense and has tried to prove he could not possibly have made so many calls, will appreciate the difficulty of this. And, without doubt, the con-trickster can easily shelter behind the errors of the computer itself, either real or fictitious.

A remarkable example of computer sleight-of-hand tactics coupled with imaginative if irregular business practice was uncovered when a British chemical company centralised the accounts for its main three divisions. The company's chief buyer and its chief computer programmer soon detected an anomaly in that division A was selling chemicals to division B without the normal 40 per cent discount for a bulk purchaser. On the strength of this discovery they launched a subsidiary company and as such claimed and secured extended credit terms and immediate payment quite apart from the 40 per cent. discount

Soon they were not only selling to sixty outside companies, but also to division B, thus undercutting their own "parent company". They made profits (on which they actually paid tax) of £150,000 in under three years. Eventually their enterprise was discovered and both men were dismissed from the company. Yet their operation was so efficient that it was incorporated as a recognised section of the company thereafter.

Although such activities come under the heading of conmanship, it can be said that not all of them are criminal or even illegal. Indeed, many individualistic exploitations of the computer system are the results of intelligent planning and a dislike of waste. The most intelligent and efficient of computer programmers or operators may get so incensed at the inefficiencies of the system which they see being ignored that they are driven to crime. Or, let us put it this way: loathing waste and seeing nothing done to prevent it, they almost instinctively take advantage of the system to eliminate some of the waste for their own ends. It cannot always be said that such conduct is necessarily immoral, let alone criminal.

Computers cost big money both to install and to maintain; when their full capacity is not taken up there is an obvious economic wastage and loss to any company or organisation. This is especially true of the communications industry and in those areas where computerology is linked with a company's telex network. Many companies who use telex for sending and receiving messages all over the world do not utilise anything like total capacity for communications. In other words, they have each day several hours of unused telex time, when the machines are idle and the firm is in effect paying for wasted time. They could, of course, quite easily and profitably "sell time" by offering telex facilities to other companies.

Sometimes this time wastage on telex is exploited by individuals. One programmer managed to run a marriage bureau in the hours when his firm's computer and telex system was unused. Starting off unsuspected by his firm at the rate of only a couple of hours each night, he was able to develop his business sufficiently to branch out on his own at a later date. It is now increasingly common for data processing managers, with spare time available on the computer, to start their own computer bureau. It is very rare indeed for the chief executives of a company to know anything about computers and they could easily be in the computer room without knowing what was going on under their very eyes.

There have been many cases in America of individuals being charged with stealing company information from a computer. In one such case the computer, which had a built-in security system, informed its owners that it was committing a robbery. More disturbing is the fact that this appeared to be "a first case" of a computer actually detecting an internal crime. One wonders how many computers are not "owning up". It is probable that today the biggest crimes of all—at least in terms of cash and cash value—are those perpetrated through the computer system.

Nor is the telephone system all that secure. There was the Great Telephone Robbery of the late 'sixties. A group of young men, some with university degrees and others with telephone engineering experience, had evolved a system for cheating the British Post Office by making calls all over the world at local rates with the use of a "bleep", or, as they called it, a "cheat box". This exploitation of a dialling-round-the-world-for-free telephone system resulted in the conviction of a number of young Britons. They had cleverly worked on the principle of obtaining their information not the hard way, but through the efforts of others. When the Britons were brought to trial, it was stated that they "have used and abused the telephone system both in the United Kingdom and abroad on an increasing and important scale, advancing at the same time not only their own, but others' knowledge of the system. For that purpose they exchanged information by letter about highly technical matters. The conspiracy had been going on from 1968 until October, 1970."

A device had been developed which defeated the Post Office system by sending signals to the Post Office machinery which would act upon them, believing them to be despatched lawfully. At the other end of the scale there was a system of cheating which consisted of a twopenny piece being attached to a fine piece of thread, thus enabling calls to be made from a public box by inserting the piece in the slot and then retrieving it. A little silver box called a "bleep box" enabled a call to be made at a local rate to almost anywhere in the world.

It was not so much the actual fraud which the case revealed which was alarming, but the indication that the system which these young people had organised enabled them to obtain a whole list of top secret numbers, including some of Government Departments and the Special Branch of the Police. If the telephone fraud racket had not been detected by the Post Office, the whole security of the country might in time have been brought to trial and it was stated in court that the fraud involved three hundred and sixty group switch centres and would cost the Post Office £400,000 to prevent such a fraud recurring in future.

18

NOTHING SUCCEEDS LIKE THE TRULY BIZARRE

DR. JOSEF GOBBELS, Hitler's propaganda genius, is said to have coined the dictum that "the bigger the lie, the more likely it is to be believed." In the sphere of conmanship it could equally be argued that the more bizarre the ploy, the surer its initiator can be of ultimate success.

In many respects this is as surprisingly true in the twentieth century as in earlier periods when widespread ingorance and supersitition enabled the credulous to be conned by any fantastic story. There was the case of an Englishman who, a few years ago, actually managed to fool several other men that he had invented the perfect aphrodisiac. There had been a few similar cases in the 1950's, mostly involving the use of dangerous drugs or commodities like cantharides, but Mr. X decided to profit from the lessons of these failures while at the same time concentrating on people who would be least likely to complain when they realised they had been conned.

He claimed that he had made his perfect aphrodisiac from an ancient secret recipe of which he alone had possession. Its great advantage was that it was absolutely safe, unlike most other aphrodisiacs, and its effect, he asserted, was that it made any man who took it irresistible to women.

One would have thought that in the 1970's such a claim would have been laughed off as a kind of April fool joke by anyone who heard it. But Mr. X's sales patter was extremely effective. Also he did not select his potential customers indiscriminately: he carefully chose them from two types, first, the wealthy who were very shy, but desperately wanted to be loved, and, secondly, from the ultra-amorous who were not particularly attractive or who had some physical defects, but lacked nothing for money. No attempt was made to sell to the average, normal heterosexual. X's sales talk went something like this: "I quite agree, old chap, that it sounds impossible. How can a pill *you* take make you irresistible to women? You will say that what you swallow cannot influence what women feel. But you see, this pill has such an effect on your personality, so boosts your ego and makes you full of well-being that women cannot fail to detect it. And then—well, just try one for a day for free. Then come back to me tomorrow and tell me how it works. If it has worked, I shall expect a payment. If not, well you haven't lost anything and there will be nothing to pay. But I am ready to bet you will want to buy a stock of the pills."

The price he charged was quite high—five pounds for the first pill, three pounds each for the next five pills and one pound per pill for any thereafter. It is probable that the pill contained a modicum of methadrine, a drug which can produce euphoric effects. Otherwise it was little more than a placebo. Mr. X had engaged some six girls who appeared to have come completely under his spell to the extent that they would do almost anything for him. If he had tried a pill out on a shy male (he always made his customers take their pills before leaving his premises), he would send one of these girls to shadow him. Somehow or other the girl would then attract the attention of the client and allow herself to be dated and, apparently, much impressed by him. Usually one simple, friendly platonic encounter was enough with this type : the shy male would be so delighted that any girl should take notice of him that he would unhesitatingly return to the salesman on the following day and request more pills.

But with the brash, over-sexed clients it was sometimes necessary for the girl chosen to follow him to acquiesce in something much more than a platonic evening out before the randy client would be convinced of the efficacy of the pill. And it was through one of the girls overplaying her part that this outrageous con-trick was eventually detected. The salesman smartly disappeared and is believed to have transferred his dubious business to Florida.

In 1975 details of another bizarre con-trick were revealed at Reading Crown Court, where on March 20th, Philip Riley, formerly a club owner at Thatcham, Berkshire, was jailed for two years for obtaining money by deception.

This twenty-nine-year-old con-trickster seems to have combined a desire for acquiring money quickly with a fondness for make-believe. He posed to the parish Roman Catholic priest, Father Francis Garlick, as a high-ranking agent in the British Secret Service who had been sent on tough underworld assignments against international communism. By swearing the priest to secrecy and making him a "lieutenant-colonel in the Secret Service", he conned large sums of money out of him over a long period. Twice he persuaded Father Garlick to say requiem masses for agents, who, he alleged, had been "killed in action".

On one occasion, Riley turned up at the presbytery with faked gunshot wounds. Another time he told Father Garlick that his cover had been "blown", that he was in dire danger and must disappear from the country immediately. He added that he had been ordered to go to Spain for safety and that because the priest was involved, he must go too. Father Garlick then supplied a thousand pounds for Riley, his wife, and two children to go to Spain for a fortnight's holiday. The priest accompanied them.

Once Father Garlick was asked to put up three hundred and fifty pounds to get an agent out of prison. None of the money the priest gave Riley came out of church funds; some of the money was his own, the rest he borrowed from friends. He made a record of all payments made to Riley which totalled £20,000. While Riley used some of the money to keep a girl friend in Oxford, it was stated in mitigation at his trial that some of the funds were used for his sick wife and that Riley had chosen this way of making a living in order to spend more time with her. Father Garlick had a nervous breakdown when he heard of Riley's arrest.

Setting up office in a splendid building in an expensive district of Los Angeles and announcing that she was about to produce a sensational new car model which would revolutionise design throughout the world, a dynamic, flamboyant and attractive saleswoman created a furore in the American motor industry in 1974. She was Elizabeth Carmichael, a widow with five children, whose long curly hair tumbled over her shoulders as she talked impressively and with the utmost confidence about her plans to hard-boiled newsmen and prospective clients. "My car is going to make me the Henry Ford of the 1980's," she declared. "Anything a man can do, I can do better. This little girl from the farmlands of Indiana is going places, Honey. I have the right idea at the psychologically right moment. By 1976 I shall be producing 250,000 cars a year."

Mrs. Carmichael had a scale model of the car, which

she called the Revette, a sleek, yellow-coloured, low-slung two-seater with something of the appearance of a miniature space-ship in its make-up. She showed the model on television and praised its qualities. When appearing on the screen, she would hold up a bunch of hundred dollar bills and announce: "That's all the car is going to cost you" (£800). And she backed up her big talk with champagne parties for the press, after which she started to sell agencies for the car, promising that very soon the first Revette would come off the production lines.

She named her company the Twentieth Century Corporation, a grandiose title which seems to have gone down well with the would-be agents who queued up to make deals with her. Options for the first few thousand cars off the production lines were snapped up. Cash flowed into the company's coffers.

Then one day disaster struck the Twentieth Century Corporation. The promotion manager was found dead in his office, shot through the head. Police inquiries revealed that he had been in prison and one of the other members of the staff was charged with his killing. Mrs. Carmichael insisted that she knew nothing at all about the backgrounds of either men. Nevertheless, to get away from the scandal, she moved to Dallas where another office, together with a factory, was opened.

But from then on the activities of the Twentieth Century Corporation were closely watched. Inquiry agents discovered that the "factory", which was to produce the Revette, was simply a delapidated warehouse full of waste material and junk. As for the Revette, the engine of this miracle car consisted solely of parts from other motor car engines and a carburettor extracted from a motor-mower. Mrs. Carmichael's "company of the century" was declared bankrupt.

Elizabeth Carmichael, however, was a jump ahead of the police who seem to have moved incredibly slowly.

Charges were made against her, but by the time police reached her apartment she had fled. Whatever money there had been she had taken with her. But an examination of her home revealed some unusual features. There were the usual feminine articles of clothing and cosmetics, but in addition were wigs, padded bras and an electric razor.

Baffled, because there was no record of anyone named Elizabeth Carmichael on their lists of wanted persons, the police worked on the theory that "she" might be a man in disguise. They took photographs of Carmichael to their photographic laboratory, had the hair and feminine decorations painted out and then re-photographed the face. This they compared with photographs in their files of wanted men. It was then that they detected a remarkable resemblance to one Jerry Dean Michael, who was wanted on charges of forgery and absconding on bail.

Jerry Dean Michael was eventually located hiding out in an apartment in Miami, still wearing women's attire.

"Are you of the male sex?" inquired the police.

"I look on myself as a woman," was the reply. "You can call me Liz."

The story of Jerry Dean Michael was that of an extraordinary transvestite who, though latterly opting for life in a female role, had actually run away from his native state of Indiana many years previously with a girl named Vivienne Barrett with whom he had produced five children. Most of the time he had lived on his wits. Apparently the transvestite problems only occurred to any marked degree in the later years and Jerry Dean, his wife and children had lived together amicably while he actually began to change his sex, first with hormone treatment. It was at this time that the car promotion stunt was embarked upon.

When Jerry Dean Michael went to prison to await trial, Vivienne, his wife, insisted that she would stand by him: "He has been a good husband and father," she said, "and he has always looked after us and shown us every consideration. We all love Liz just as much as we love Jerry, and the kids call him Mother Liz, while I'm just plain Mom. I suppose you could say we are like sisters rather than man and wife."

One of the most gigantic, global con-tricks perpetrated in recent years was what became known as the "Six S. Job", or the Siam, Singapore, Somali, Soviet Sugar Swindle. This netted more than £2,500,000 in the 1970's and was operated from a small office in Bangkok where telephones rang endlessly, but nobody answered. It was here that the huge deal was planned and in which scheme 9,313 tons of sugar totally disappeared.

Even now members of Scotland Yard's Fraud Squad, who became indirectly involved, are baffled as to how so small a syndicate pulled off such a coup. The complex swindle, which involved five countries, can be traced back to a deserted room in the Bangkok office rented by the Eastern Development Corporation. The man who master-minded it was a mysterious Mr. Chern, an enigmatic, quick-thinking and impressive businessman who had friends in high places all over the world.

In the early 1970's there had been a shortage of sugar in various places in the world and the Somali Government was particularly concerned about this. The Somalis ordered 10,000 tons of sugar and completed their deal without checking on the cargo ordered. To finance this deal the Somalis turned to Moscow where they had been promised assistance in an emergency. The Russians, normally ultra-cautious in such deals, arranged for the Narodny Bank to issue a cheque for 5,900,000 American dollars, while at the same time being taken in by a forged lading bill.

It was a company known as the Crescent Impex of Singapore which first indicated to the desperate Somali

Government that they could supply the sugar. But, they said, first they would have to negotiate the deal with the Eastern Development Company in Bangkok. Crescent Impex got the go-ahead signal from the Somali Government to act as middle-man and then signed an agreement with Eastern Development's Mr. Chern.

With the money provided by the Russians all seemed well. But the Somalis should have been alerted to possible dangers when Crescent Impex specifically requested that the letter of credit should be made out to a newly formed Singapore company. This company had only been established in May, 1974, with a paid-up capital of two dollars. There were only two members of its board, the brother and wife of a Singapore consultant who worked for Crescent Impex. But the Somalis had not looked into this at the time.

The Singapore company delivered a bill of lading plus certificates of quality and quantity to the Moscow Narodny Bank (all faked), which authorised the letter of credit to be cashed and indicated that 10,000 tons of sugar had been loaded at Ko Sichang, a port 45 miles south of Bangkok, for delivery to the Somali Trading Agency at Berbera.

Originally the cargo was supposed to have been put aboard a Liberian-registered ship owned by the Taiship Company, which was linked to the Consolidated Cosmopolitan Line, an unlisted company in Bangkok of which not only was Mr. Chern a member, but had the same address as the Eastern Development Corporation. But in September, 1974, the Somali Government was informed by cable that the sugar cargo would not be put aboard the Liberian-registered ship, but the 4,205-ton *Lord Byron*, owned by a Greek company known as Valia Oceanica Armodora. The master of the ship, which had just arrived in Bangkok, was told that the cargo would be loaded overnight before they sailed, but that the documents, including the bill of lading, would not be completed before sailing time but that they would be sent on to the next port of call, Berbera.

A cargo of sugar was in fact loaded at Bangkok, but this amounted to only 687 tons, not the 10,000 the Somali Government had paid for with the loan from Moscow. So the *Lord Byron* arrived in Berbera to be greeted by highly displeased Somali officials and was immediately impounded while inquiries were made. Several days later a cable arrived in Berbera stating that the sugar was still in Bangkok in the care of the We Hua Trading Company, agents of the Consolidated Cosmopolitan Line. The only address for this company was once more the small back room office rented by the mysterious Mr. Chern. But nobody at that office admitted any knowledge of Mr. Chern and the Siamese Government informed the Somalis that such a deal as they had mentioned was not permissible in Siam. The Siamese Government only permitted two companies to export sugar and neither of these companies was associated with Mr. Chern.

It was a gigantic con-trick and an even bigger mystery than most. The Russians were furious and somebody must have been severely reprimanded at the Narodny Bank. The Singapore charterers said something must have gone wrong en route as they believed the sugar was loaded in Bangkok. A British insurance company was involved because they had arranged a million pound policy for the ship.

"UFO's, why they are here; who they have come for; when they will leave. If you have ever entertained the idea that there might be a real physical level in space beyond earth's confines, you will want to attend this meeting at the Bayshore Inn Hotel on Tuesday."

This was the handwritten poster which in September 1975 announced a meeting to be held in the tiny fishing village of Waldport in Oregon. Some 300 people turned up, including holiday-makers, fishermen and casual visitors. They were received by a man and a woman who claimed that very shortly they would be leaving earth on a space-ship. The man announced this quite calmly and added that their mission was to come in human form from "the next kingdom" and to save those who accepted their doctrine. Quoting from the *Book of Revelations*, always apparently a favourite source of inspiration for the more eccentric of our spell-weavers, he declared that both of them would be "assassinated and reincarnated within three days, after which we shall ascend in a cloud".

This somewhat obscure message seemed to imply that the pair would then return to earth, pick up their followers in an Unidentified Flying Object and fly them off to paradise. Then came the sales talk. The gist of this was that anybody in the audience who really wished to "follow the call" could do so, if only they would abandon their earthly possessions. What they held out to those who would agree to throw in their lot with "The Two" (as the man and woman became known) was a trip to eternity on a flying saucer.

One person who attended the meeting said afterwards: "He seemed to be describing something like one of Kurt Vonnegut's imaginary planets in those science-fiction stories".

Another said: "We were clearly told that sex was forbidden by this cult, or whatever they represented. Recruits were informed that part of the preparation for ascending to the higher plane of paradise was to spend time in a kind of sexless purgatory on earth".

Part of the dogma was that friction was needed to "transcend the human form" and that followers would be grouped in pairs who would not be expected to get along. Thus a homosexual must travel with a beautiful girl and an introvert with a gregarious type. Children would have to be given away because they were not ready for "the next kingdom".

A woman who attended another meeting of the cult in San Francisco at a later date said: "They don't permit married couples to live together. They don't allow any human commitments of any kind. People have to give up all their possessions and all their relationships".

Probably the Waldport meeting would have attracted little attention except for mild amusement, some guffaws and local gossip, but for an unexpected sequel. It was suddenly reported that twenty of those who had attended the meeting and had been persuaded to join the cult had mysteriously disappeared. There was even more consternation when it was learned that some of the twenty had given away their homes, property and even their children before disappearing.

The sinister word "assassination" had been mentioned by the mysterious "Two". Was this an imaginative fraud scheme involving a flying saucer and with hints of mass murder?

Another meeting was scheduled for San Jose, California, early in October, 1975, and, as a result of press reports of the disappearance of the people in Oregon, a crowd of five hundred turned up. They were extremely angry when the mysterious "Two" failed to appear. Inquiries then revealed that this crusade into outer space had first been heard of in the spring when thirty followers of the cult set out for California in cars and caravans, camping in the mountains not far from San Francisco while other meetings were held at the university campuses of Berkeley and Stanford.

In mid-August the Two Apostles from Outer Space had taken part in a radio programme from San Jose, in which they explained some of their aims. They claimed to be "on the same vibrational level as Jesus Christ" and said that they travelled from planet to planet on flying saucers spreading the word, and that soon they would lead their followers from Mother Earth. But first, they said, the followers must undergo an intensive training course to fit them for paradise.

At the Waldport meeting those who had agreed to take part in "this great spiritual adventure" had been told to give up their property and children and follow "The Two" to a camp in Colorado some thousand miles to the east.

Douglas Greene, the superintendent of the dam at Bonny Dam, Burlington, Colorado, said afterwards: "They arrived all right and they camped near the reservoir. They said they were heading for Nebraska to meet up with a caravan party from somewhere else and that they were going to another and better world on another planet".

On October 13th police at Portland (Oregon) added three more people to the list of those who had vanished from Oregon to follow the mysterious couple who had promised them a UFO trip. This brought the total missing to twenty-three. Melvin Gibson, the criminal investigator for the Oregon State Police, said he had obtained copies of letters written by a young woman from the Corvallie area of Oregon who had definitely joined "The Two". He said the letters were dated September 22nd and 26th and that they were posted in Colorado.

Parents of some young people who had decided to join the cult had flown half way across America to try to talk them out of it. But the youngsters had disappeared without trace. There was an outcry that the authorities should carry out immediate investigations and a search for the missing people. Deputy Sheriff Ron Sutton, who was put in charge of the inquiry, said that some of those who had disappeared were "hippies and drifters with no local relatives. There was nothing we could do. I believe folk were scared into believing something. But that's not a crime. It is all too weird. I talked to some of these kids before they left. I'm told that at least one couple, Ron and Judy Green, gave their young children away before they left, but I can't prove it. A guy called Dan Staggs, a nursery gardener, left his job and signed over the title to his house. He should have known better than that. He was forty-three.

"Others have given up apartments and homes. One girl, whose first name is Charity, just left her baby with friends. She told them she was expecting the Second Coming."

One Oregon newspaper columnist suggested that the "Trips to Paradise" cult was a hoax concocted by two students who were writing a thesis entitled 'Psychological Reactions to Panic in a Small American Town". But by the time several months had passed and other meetings had been held, it was generally agreed that this was something much bigger than a hoax and that far too much time and money had been spent in pursuing the objectives.

The mystery of the identity of "The Two" took rather longer to unravel. It seemed that they altered their names according to the locations at which they held their meetings and whether they were addressing romantically-minded students or adults. But there was nothing particularly sinister about the pseudonyms they gave themselves—Peter and Fanta, Bo and Peep, the Pied Pipers of Space, Winnie and Pooh, Chip and Dale, He and She and Guinea and Pig.

Their true identities were, in fact, much less enchanting, though still mildly absurd in their nomenclature. "The Two" were ultimately identified as Herff Applewhite and Bonnie Trusdale Nettles, a neatly-dressed, middle-aged couple of sober appearance and life-style who had formerly taught philosophy at Houston, Texas. But nobody seemed able to track them down. From time to time in the later months of 1975 they were seen at meetings and heard to have enrolled more followers. But as soon as some investigator came on the scene they had moved elsewhere.

Among the twenty-three who disappeared after attending the Waldport meeting was Dan Staggs, a nurseryman about to open his own business. He had recently had a divorce. His seventy-two-year-old mother, Mrs. Hilda Eaton, told how her son had vanished: "It was a Sunday evening when he dropped in with some friends on their way home from the meeting. They said they had heard some pretty heavy stuff, but I gathered they were interested. Then by the following Thursday Dan had gone".

Dan had not only disappeared, he had signed a legal deed giving his three-bedroomed house to Miss Christine Carlson, of Springfield, Oregon. Miss Carlson told a reporter that "he woke me up one night at my parents' place and gave me the deeds. I realise I couldn't be luckier, but I wouldn't have accepted it if I hadn't been convinced he was absolutely sincere and positive about leaving. He was always a very searching person, a deep thinker".

Another one who vanished was Anne Miller, a twenty-four-year-old artist who made stained-glass windows. Her father searched for her in vain in Texas and New Mexico where members of the cult were reported to have been sighted. Her step-mother, Mrs. Kay Miller, said: "It's worse than having a loved one die, to be grieving for someone you know is still alive, but who won't get in touch."

All that was heard from Anne was a farewell telephone call to say she was off for paradise.

A young Oregon couple, known only by their first names of Christian and Liz, left when Liz was nine months' pregnant. They were believed to have joined the cult and Liz had her baby in a tent in Colorado and then gave it away. The delivery was attended by Mrs. Jackie Leonard, wife of an eye specialist from Colorado. He told the press that his wife had also disappeared along with Christian and Liz. "Yes, she joined the cult all right," was his bitter comment. "Can you imagine a lovely lady like her running around with a crazy group like that? I personally wouldn't kill them, but some day somebody will . . ."

Yet all is not nearly so sinister as it appeared to be when the first twenty-three so dramatically vanished. For in January, 1976, Dan Staggs re-appeared as surprisingly as he had vanished. He announced that he had returned to make a drive for recruits for the cult. He was rather vague as to what the cult stood for, other than that it promised salvation, but he said he fully intended to rejoin "The Two" and make the trip to paradise. He called on Miss Carlson, the woman to whom he had given away his home, and collected a frying-pan, which he took away with him.

"He looked quite well and said he was happy," declared Miss Carlson afterwards. "He refused to call on his mother and I know this upset her very much. Dan said that he had to sever all old ties and that it would be painful to see her again. But he did say that the prospect of salvation when he took off in the UFO, or whatever is is, for Outer Space would more than compensate for these earthly matters. It was only a brief visit, and he was soon on his way again."

All members of the cult are apparently urged to bring cooking utensils, tents, sleeping-bags and plenty of warm clothing for the nomadic life which they lead while preparing for salvation. Oddly enough, Dan Stagg gave away his bicycle but kept his car. Maybe he wanted the car for his recruiting drive.

From time to time there have been drop-outs whether simply from society itself, or drop-outs from the cult as well, has not always been clear—who have given news of the Outer Spacers. They say that the membership west of the Rockies might be as high as a thousand. But then the west coast of America from Oregon to Mexico is full of devotees of weird, off-beat cults. But it just so happens that this particular one is less explicable than most. There is no evidence of anything criminal about it, nothing alarming about the disappearances—at least not since Dan Stagg made his brief return—and no indication that anyone is making vast sums of money out of it, or gaining a harem as Charles Manson did, or exploiting the followers in the manner in which Prince and Smyth-Pigott did a century or more previously. Those who agree to join bring some money with them: they do not literally give away *all* their possessions. What happens when it runs out is anyone's guess.

No one can say how the cult will progress, or how it will end, how soon disillusionment will seep through the ranks of the followers of the Pied Pipers of Space. It would seem to be a most unusual example of a kind of hysterical, self-conning society, with the conned conning themselves as much as being conned by the conners. It is the nearest one has got to the ultimate in conmanship, a form, if you like, of telepathic conmanship, a world in which we all con ourselves. To this extent, it is a highly dangerous development in human society and one which could be manipulated unscrupulously.

Yet the Outer Spacers certainly have not been manipulated unscrupulously as far as one can tell. What they are doing is of their own free will. In the past there were people who, with a little guidance from other make-believers, sought their own utopias on earth rather in the manner of the Lotus Eaters of legend. Some found their paradise in black magic, or a belief in fairies. Today, the attention of their 1970's counterparts is to Outer Space. Carl Jung, in a book on flying saucers, claims that the world-wide sightings of UFO's may be the expression of "a wave of hope in a re-appearance of Christ", the suggestion being that flying saucers have an objective existence.

BIBLIOGRAPHY

ANONYMOUS : *Sketches of Imposture*, London, 1837.

BOUTARIC, E. : *Correspondance secrete inedité de Louis XV*, II.

CARLYLE, Thomas : *Cagliostro and the Diamond Necklace*.

CHATTERTON, Thomas: The Rowley Poems; see the account written under Chatterton's pseudonym of *Dunelmus-Bristoliensis* in *Felix Farley's Bristol Journal*, 1768.

HALLIWELL, James Orchard: *The Private Diary of Dr. John Dee and the Catalogue of His Library of Manuscripts*, John Bowyer Nichols & Sons, London, printed for the Camden Society, 1842.

JOHNSON, James and MILLER, Floyd : *The Man Who Sold the Eiffel Tower*, W. H. Allen, London, 1962.

LANG, Andrew : *Cock Lane and Commonsense*, London, 1894.

MACKAY, Charles : *Memoirs of Extraordinary Popular Delusions and the Madness of Crowds*, George Routledge & Sons, London, 1869.

MANNINGHAM, R. : *Diary of Attendance upon Mary Toft, the rabbet-breeder*, London, 1727.

MILLAR, Ronald : *The Piltdown Man*, London, 1972.

NICOLAIEVSKY, Boris : *Azeff: The Spy, Russian Terrorist & Police Stool*.

PSALMANAZAR, George: *An Historical and Geographical Description of Formosa*, 1704, and *Memoirs*, 1764.

ST. ANDRE, N. : *Extraordinary Delivery of Rabbets, perform'd by J. Howard*, London, 1727.

WAITE, Arthur E.: *Alchemical Writings of Edward Kelly*, London, 1893.

WATTS, Theodore: article in *Ward's English Poets*, Vol III, 1880.

WEINER, J. S., OAKLEY, K. P. and LE GROS CLARK, W. E.: *Bulletin of the British Museum* (*Natural History*), Vol. II, No. 3, 1953.

Also consulted: *Dictionary of National Biography*; the Public Record Office; *The Harvard Crimson*, 24 November, 1953 (regarding the Piltdown hoax); *The True Briton*, 1874 (regarding the Tichborne Case; *The Times*, *Sunday Times* of London; *Daily Telegraph*, *Sunday Telegraph* of London; *Empire News*; *Evening Standard* of London; *Daily Mail* of London; *Sussex Archaeological Collections*, 1912; the *Kaspar Hauser Papers*, Munich.

Acknowledgement is gratefully made to the following for research in France, Germany and the U.S.A. respectively: Mr. Frank Dorsey, of Yvelines, France; Fraulein Hilde Hoffman, Munich; and Mr. Eric H. Wiseman, New York.

INDEX